Big
Mall

Big Mall

SHOPPING FOR MEANING

Kate Black

COACH HOUSE BOOKS, TORONTO

first edition

Published with the generous assistance of the Canada Council for the Arts and the Ontario Arts Council. Coach House Books also acknowledges the support of the Government of Canada through the Canada Book Fund and the Government of Ontario through the Ontario Book Publishing Tax Credit.

LIBRARY AND ARCHIVES CANADA CATALOGUING IN PUBLICATION

Title: Big mall : shopping for meaning / by Kate Black.
Names: Black, Kate (Kate Grace), author.
Identifiers: Canadiana (print) 20230556744 | Canadiana (ebook) 2023055685X | ISBN 9781552454725 (softcover) | ISBN 9781770567825 (EPUB) | ISBN 9781770567832 (PDF)
Subjects: LCSH: West Edmonton Mall (Edmonton, Alta.) | LCSH: Shopping malls—Social aspects. | LCSH: Shopping—Psychological aspects.
Classification: LCC HF5430.6.C3 B53 2024 | DDC 381/.1109712334—dc23

Introduction

Recently, immediately after buying a twenty-three-dollar stir-fry soaking in canola oil, as I shook from low blood sugar and panicked about having no money, I tweeted: 'when i go to the mall i feel connected to the great symphony of human experience!'

When I go to the mall, I usually want to leave right away.

When I go to the mall, I feel like I'm on the tip of becoming myself.

I find it difficult to pin down one clean thought about visiting the mall. What I do know is that, right now, I'm haunted by the feeling that my life will not get much better than this, which makes me both grateful and afraid.

———

When we go to the mall, we're entering a mistake. Or at least a miscalculation. I mean, look around. Not much of this screams, 'God's plan!'

In one of the many contradictions in the mall's origin story, its inventor, Victor Gruen, hated cars. Gruen, a Jewish architect, fled Nazi-occupied Austria for New York City in 1938. He soon settled in Los Angeles, where shopping was a complete perversion from the storefronts he designed and the high streets he loved in his native Vienna. As Gruen began picking up more work across the country, he found car-cluttered, billboard-lined Miracle Miles everywhere he went, a loneliness loud enough to inspire invention. He first put words to his vision in a 1943 issue of *Architectural Forum*, which asked a handful of well-known architects to envisage how buildings would change once the war ended. Gruen's prediction was a manifestation. Soon, he wrote, shopping would be turned outside-in: disparate stores would be compiled into a single building, connected by covered walkways to post offices and libraries. They would be called shopping centres. Visiting them would be restful, even life-affirming.

By the time his first indoor mall, Southdale Center in Edina, Minnesota, opened its doors in 1956, Gruen's qualms about American urban design had only magnified. To accommodate the millions of men returning from war and the resulting baby boom, government-insured loans and low interest rates triggered the growth of the suburbs. This movement, augmented by the fact that just about everyone owned a car, siphoned consumers from city centres and the remaining life from shopping itself. A trip to the store meant just that: driving your car to a stand-alone shop or strip mall and buying what you came to buy before hopping back in and heading home, often alone.

Southdale Center, at first, was regarded as a triumphant intervention. Its opening triggered a nationwide mediastorm; *Time* magazine touted it as a 'pleasure dome with parking.' With Southdale, Gruen didn't just bring the high street completely indoors; he controlled the climate with air conditioning and made it beautiful with a garden, an atrium, and modern escalators. Shopping, he envisioned, would no longer be a chore, but a relaxing break from the other necessities of life, and Southdale was a first-of-its-kind space in which to gather outside of the single-family home or the workplace. Gruen also saw the mall, of course, as a surefire way to make money. At the large, partially outdoor shopping centres built before Southdale, revenue sagged during rainy or too-hot days. They were altogether impossible in Midwest winters. Riding on the apparent success of Southdale, and the suburb boom that enabled it, more than 250 shopping centres were built across the United States in the following ten years.

The shopping centre was only meant to be the starting point in a larger connected development. According to Gruen's master plan, the remaining 379 acres bought by Southdale's developers would be filled with the other vital elements of a community: a school, a post office, medical and dental offices, a library. Throughout his career, Gruen proselytized the social power of commerce. Later, once the suburbanization of North America drained foot traffic from urban centres, he similarly proposed malls as a solution. If we could just bring shoppers back to the city, he thought, the city could be as lively as the suburbs. And if we just put malls in the city, people wouldn't need to leave the city to go to the mall. Among his complexities, Gruen was a wealthy socialist, already hailing from a rich family before becoming one of the world's most sought-after architects. He believed that commerce was the key to a vibrant community, urban or not. Cities, especially with the gallerias back home in Vienna, got their vitality from having shoppers out and about, browsing store windows, meeting with a friend at a café.

Most people who write about Gruen agree that his visions ultimately failed. Malls sucked life out of the cities, and putting malls in downtowns, where their target clientele rarely lived, didn't bring life back. The mall and its giant parking lot were the only parts of the Southdale plan that stuck. Once it opened, the value of surrounding land skyrocketed; the developers, naturally, sold it off to make way for even more rows of houses, instead of the other amenities Gruen had imagined. Ever since, this pattern has become commonplace. Mall developers buy up much more land than they need. Shoppers come, driving up the value of the neighbouring areas; developers sell the excess, making a fortune. Now gracing virtually every city on the planet, Gruen's vision of the mall clearly took off – just not how he had expected.

He would come to resent the gargantuan structures built in Southdale's image.

'I refuse to pay alimony for those bastard developments,' Gruen said in 1978, two years before his death. 'They destroyed our cities.'

In the final years of his life, Gruen returned to Vienna, his home and architectural muse. He was met with a dark irony: Shopping City Süd, one of Europe's largest malls, was being built in the countryside, cursing his beloved city with the same cruel fate he had tried to design away. This grand vision and poetic downfall has established Gruen as a folkloric figure, a cautionary tale for enterprising men who contain multitudes.

Judging by American think pieces alone, you'd be led to believe that malls – all of them, everywhere – are dying. And although it would be poetic to say that malls are finally following their reluctant creator to the grave almost fifty years later, it just wouldn't be true.

The twenty-first-century mall blight targets only a certain shopping centre: a quarter of the thousand or so scattered across the loosely populated autopias of the United States. Mostly, shoppers stopped coming after the big anchor department stores, like JCPenney and Sears, tanked and shut down operations in smaller locations. And while online shopping still hasn't completely replaced in-person shopping, Amazon becomes a lot more attractive when your community mall doesn't have what you're looking for.

Many of these malls have refused to go down without a fight. In small communities, malls can become vital community hubs, home to libraries and throngs of walking seniors, maybe the one place to meet with a friend for a drink. People hold protests to try to save malls; some go even further. In 2019, presidential candidate Andrew Yang proposed the $6 billion American Mall Act to save them. Although it never came to fruition, the act would have provided financial incentives to smaller retailers and real-estate developers to fill the rapidly emptying spaces that threatened to close at least three hundred small malls by 2024.

But other small malls, by the time they're demolished, have been empty long enough to have evolved into an aesthetic and discursive phenomenon of their own: witness the r/deadmalls subreddit, YouTube channels dedicated to simulating the sound of eighties music playing in an empty mall, countless articles of cultural criticism examining the mournful nostalgia and fascination. Talk about the death of American malls coincided with the death of a certain America, waving goodbye to an institution people didn't even know they could be nostalgic for, leaving a physical metaphor in its wake.

A lot of America's mall death is attributable to its initial verve in building them. American urban planning has always been less beholden to local governments and zoning laws, which allowed malls to grow in the United States four times faster than in Canada. The United States currently has twice as much retail space per capita as Europe.

The global economy has evolved dramatically since the Southdale Centre made its mark. Following suit, people's shopping looks different now, too. But malls as a category are not dying.

Take a look anywhere else – Canada, Europe, Asia, the Middle East – and the story plays out differently. The reasons behind this are complex; each continent, let alone the countries and cities therein, has developed consumer economies on unique terms. What unites them all, however, is that the successful malls in these areas have transcended merely functioning as a place to buy things. They have become massive spectacles, housing ski slopes and movie theatres, zoos and waterparks. More depressingly, the mall is a shelter, rising to meet the needs of an increasingly unbearable climate. In areas of Asia and the Middle East, the mall is the only place for people to enjoy the comfort of air conditioning.

So, really big malls, like the one I grew up at, are doing better than ever. When a mall is a people magnet to the nearest city (or five), the good, exclusive stores have no reason to leave. Even then, a megamall isn't maimed by losing a couple retailers to a Walmart being built down the road. Some become so big that their main event isn't even shopping – it's riding a roller coaster or getting drunk on an indoor patio. They're inventing social experiences, all but exactly what Gruen once dreamed.

——————

I come from Edmonton, Alberta. More accurately, I come from St. Albert, a suburb of Edmonton that you're even less likely to have heard about. Even using the word *suburb* to describe St. Albert, as if Edmonton proper is the pinnacle of urbanism, feels silly. Edmonton, in reality, is baggy, like a canvas punctured by neighbourhoods all linked by half-hour drives and strip malls. It's sliced in half by a wide river populated by prehistoric sturgeon and celebrated by local boosters as the most interesting tourist destination imaginable. Edmonton has beautiful prairie summers, followed by literally one week of autumn, before descending into a deep freeze for most of the year. Edmonton is huge and defies my ability to describe it. I left seven years ago and won't move back; I can't stand when people from other parts of the country dismiss it.

Edmonton has a chip on its shoulder, which can feel endearing once you're out, but irritating, even quite heavy, when you live there. Mordecai Richler once called it boring, and the local psyche has apparently never felt peace since. The city's slogan, City of Champions, was rendered cheaply ironic after Wayne Gretzky was traded to the Los Angeles Kings in 1988. Maybe that's where Edmonton got its self-esteem problems from – an entire municipality's dads in eternal grief – or maybe it has something to do with the insecurity bred from being tied to the oil sands' boom-and-bust economy, the identity crisis of a politically progressive city surrounded by conservative strongholds. During my undergrad, a combination of these elements culminated in a cultural moment where everyone wore shirts that said 'STILL IN EDMONTON.' The shirts revealed what felt too crass to say out loud: staying felt less inevitable than leaving.

I moved to Vancouver after graduating from university and quickly learned that the only thing people seem to know about my hometown is its biggest mall. (Technically it's our biggest mall, if you're in North America.) When I told Vancouverites where I was from, hardly anyone asked why I left. Instead, I was met with what resembled condolences, then congratulations for choosing a better life for myself, then a story about the one time they visited West Edmonton Mall as a child. The story often goes: They were a kid and were visiting family in the area. Their uncle worked for Enbridge or something. They probably went to Galaxyland, the world's largest indoor theme park, or the World Waterpark, the world's largest (not to brag!) waterpark. If they were rich or lucky, they would have stayed at a themed room in the Fantasyland Hotel: the hilariously insensitive African Theme Room or, my personal white whale, the Space Room, outfitted with a hot tub and a purple galaxy for a ceiling. I still feel jealous when people tell me they have stayed at the hotel – I never have, so it feels like they've stolen my Edmonton-adjacent valour, like they know my home, my whole personality, better than I do.

Millions of people have known West Edmonton Mall in one way or another. On busy days, its foot traffic surpasses the population of the third-largest city in the province. But if you're from Edmonton, you know the mall by its magnetic pull of personal and collective memory. Our childhoods were spent shopping, attending birthday parties, and loitering in what was once the biggest mall in the world. One man has dedicated a YouTube channel to detailing the mall's history since its opening in 1981 and raving about its constant new offerings: the swan boats you can ride across the mall's massive lagoon, a Bubba Gump Shrimp Company, a virtual-reality theme park. On Reddit, people love talking about how the mall looked and felt better in their own personal heyday. They miss the original location of the bronze whale statue, whose dirty-coin-smelling mouth you could climb inside before it was moved to make room for men to sit in front of Victoria's Secret. They wish they could feel the heat of the fire-breathing animatronic dragon in the movie theatre on their faces one more time, even though it used to scare the shit out of them. They have noticed that the mall is not as humid as it used to be, and humid was better.

Every time I talk to someone about the mall, I learn something new about it. Like, the fact that a friend of mine was mugged at the all-ages rave in Galaxyland, and a friend of a different friend was stabbed there. Or that every dolphin born in the mall died shortly thereafter, and the mall's lagoons once had more operational submarines than the Royal Canadian Navy. Someone's finger was torn off on one of the waterslides in the waterpark, which is likely the only place in Alberta where you can see a tropical species of cockroach. Or so the legend goes.

When describing the sheer size and importance of the mall to people who are not from Edmonton, the main fact any of us will probably tell you is that people have died there. Memorably: three, in a roller coaster crash at Galaxyland, one fact among the many that weigh the mall down into a story heavier than a pure capitalist fairy tale. The mall can have a shadowy aura, a feeling of something being not quite right, if only because of the stories we've heard, memorized, and retold about it.

In 2004, West Edmonton Mall lost its title as the largest mall in the world. Today, it's not even the busiest mall in Canada (Toronto's Eaton Centre has nearly double the number of annual visitors). Still, I cannot imagine a bigger space. At different points in my life, I've wished to erase the mall from my past and trade it for a more interesting coming-of-age story. Like, growing up wealthier in a cool, big city. Or poorer on a farm. At the time, I was not aware of any great children's literature romanticizing becoming yourself in a mid-size suburban development; this place that is so amenable to a mall also lacks the constraint (the struggle) necessary for a good narrative arc. Before they were turned into McMansions, canola fields stretched out on either side of my neighbourhood. Each time I passed them in the back seat of a car, I dreamed about swapping lives with Laura Ingalls Wilder, trading in my Neopets for what looked like the most authentic experience of living. Fearing the elements, falling asleep in a meadow, having a meadow to fall asleep in. I didn't know Laura Ingalls Wilder had been dead for a very long time.

———

For anyone with moderate social awareness, it's not hard to feel bad about malls. You know, the whole 'it represents every-thing wrong about the world,' if your beliefs about what's wrong about the world touch broadly on capitalism, consumerism, colonialism, climate change, or loud noises. Malls aren't just a metaphor for the neo-liberal American dream – they are a manifestation of its policies.

After World War II, Western governments shrunk their handouts, as they shifted responsibility for areas of tradi-tional welfare-state oversight over to the free market. The underlying theory bloomed before achieving its recognizable political form in the seventies, in reaction to the domestic danger (or global existential threat) of big, isolated govern-ments or, even worse, global communist alliances outside of the Western world's purview. Especially in the United States, the resulting relaxation of planning and real estate laws made it possible for developers to eat up farmland and churn out never-before-seen profit. Land was a commodity to be bought and sold – this wasn't a new idea. What was significant, however, was the growing trust in industry to manage what was once more firmly under the public domain. The idea that private businesses could manage resources more effectively than the public would stick around for a while – and depending on who you talk to, it doesn't show any signs of leaving.

Along the way, neo-liberalism morphed into a morality – governments ditched social-service spending to leave the market in charge, ultimately failing any of us who haven't taken sufficient hold of those mythical bootstraps. Although malls didn't cause populations to sprawl out and away from downtown cores, early mall architects (including Gruen) sold developers on racist and otherwise xenophobic rhetoric: finally, a place to shop and walk with ease, without downtown's blight of poverty and delinquency.

Malls came of age alongside the informal definition of *community* as it is often used today: the name of the housing development where you live with your spouse and kids, in a row of homes occupied by demographically similar spouses and kids. In imagination and on paper, malls became our new town squares. If we define neo-liberalism as the ideology of people's entire lives taking place in the marketplace, the mall makes for a pretty perfect metaphor.

Malls also play an active role in reproducing neo-liberalism's political-consciousness-crushing effects. For many of us, going to the mall is the most urban experience we'll have without going on vacation; if you're of the 82 per cent of Canadians who drive to work, the mall is the closest you'll get to experiencing a true cross-section of your own municipality. It may be the only place in your everyday life where you could feasibly get lost, but any mirage of public freedom offered by the mall is just that. In malls, after all, we can't protest. We can sit down and eat but have to stand up and continue shopping when we're done. Especially if you're a racialized person, experiencing the mall without contributing to its productivity will have you escorted off the premises, even banned for life.

The mall, then, physically represents how our current economic system crushes any hope for its people to demand better. It is very hard for conflict to make itself visible here – in the 'here' of the mall and the 'here' seemingly everywhere surrounding it. Our environment is purposefully oriented around consumption; it's been this way for longer than we can remember. Of course all of this seems inevitable. Or, even if we can picture otherwise, this all still seems like the best option.

Every mall's origin story parallels that of our lives' entanglement with economy. I would argue, for example, that West Edmonton Mall would not have existed in its larger-than-life form without the 1973 oil crisis. When the United States supported Israel in the Yom Kippur War, Middle Eastern and North African countries cut off their supply of cheap oil to Western allies like Canada. In response, Canada super-powered its own domestic oil-production capacity in Alberta. For the province, it ushered in a massive oil boom.

It was perfect timing for the Ghermezian family. After the war, Jacob 'Papa' Ghermezian immigrated from Iran to Canada with his wife and four sons and their rug-trading business. They also brought with them the know-how of having developed political influence and a small real-estate empire in their home country (Jacob claimed to have hosted the 1943 Tehran Conference in his own apartment complex). In 1964, the Ghermezians established their own conglomerate, Triple Five Group, which specialized in buying up hotels, office buildings, and, anticipating an oil boom, hundreds of acres of farmland. By 1974, they owned more private land than anyone else in the province. There wasn't any oil in it, but that didn't matter. The Ghermezians made a fortune by selling their real estate back to the city for development, landing them enough capital to realize their biggest dream yet: the biggest mall in the world. Today, Triple Five Group owns the three largest malls in North America: West Edmonton Mall, the Mall of America, and the American Dream.

West Edmonton Mall, then, is inseparable from the broader history of resource extraction. This is only magnified when you consider how oil seeps into so many parts of the province's imagination. In 2013, the mall estimated that 15 per cent of its shoppers came from Fort McMurray, the city focalizing the oil and gas industry four and a half hours north of Edmonton. In the past few decades, Fort Mac has grown out of its boomtown roots and now has malls of its own. But West Edmonton Mall is the closest they'll get to real luxury in the likes of Coach, Balenciaga, Tiffany, and Louis Vuitton; it's still a veritable shopping magnet for people working up north, and the rest of the 100,000 or so who work in the industry. If the main driver of this work – often in the cold, away from family, for two weeks straight – is material reward, West Edmonton Mall is the best place to realize it.

The mall couldn't be more Albertan. The mall, too, feels like a world completely on its own. Especially in the winter – specifically the *Edmonton* winter, where the wind chill makes facial expressions physically painful and orients my priorities to those of a domesticated animal, willing to do anything to feel comfortable. I'll idle a car for half an hour to feel my hands again. I'll white-knuckle it down an icy ring road just to go to the mall, if only to walk around an indoor space that's not my house. There's a punishing walk through the parking lot – thousands of other people had the same idea, only two hours earlier – but the warmth of the mall melts into my limbs the moment I open its doors. A humidity emanates from underneath the waterpark and the grease in the food courts, and I don't even care where the heat comes from, where it goes. In this moment, I'm only interested in regaining sensation.

Inevitably, reality re-enters the fantasy. More than once, I have seen forest-fire smoke hang over the mall skylights. Below them are two art installations: dozens of amber-and-gold glass oil droplets dangling from the ceiling, dripping onto an immense bronze statue of three men drilling for oil. I've started doing this thing where I try to trick myself into thinking that the smoke is just the sun setting, and that it's not actually this dark outside in the middle of the afternoon. But the truth is all over the place. You can literally smell it in the air: we're running out of time, and I am not helping.

———

And yet I cannot separate myself from it, this deranged memory palace of my life!

People in Vancouver have made fun of me for constantly mentioning where I am from. I announce this fact about myself compulsively, as if to contextualize a detectable quality about me that Edmonton somehow explains away. I must do it to meet others like me. When I find them – and I often do – we talk about the mall with the same fixation, as if it is our actual hometown. Usually, the eyes of people around us start to glaze over, but I can't stop. I'm trying to get to the bottom of an idea. Talking about where I am from feels less like telling a story than it does performing an excavation. Toward an answer, I guess. Each time, I get closer to figuring it out, but I haven't quite gotten it yet. I'm not sure what the question is, either.

I guess I am interested in understanding why something so stupid has informed my whole life. I mean the mall, but I also mean everything else: the history, the economy, the forces of human nature that made all these problems and that also made me. I don't like the particular moment where God, or history, or whoever, has dropped me. Would it have been better if I had been dropped on another place? I spend a lot of time trying to capture the problem, to pinpoint the specific point of friction between myself and the world so I can dedicate the rest of my time to resolving it. Every aspect of how this life works, I continue to find, is out of sync with what life should be about. But it is so beyond me. It makes as much sense as a family of dolphins living in a city covered in snow, across from a cinnamon bun kiosk and a life-size model of Christopher Columbus's flagship, Ke$ha's voice floating through the air.

I have tried detaching myself from engaging at all, and it was the closest thing to death. I can't opt out of living a life manipulated by living here, under all these conditions. I can't opt out of thinking about it, either. My real world, for better or for worse, has meant conceiving of my womanhood in a Hollister and watching my unrequited love make out with other people in the wave pool. My real world is a big mall.

I began writing a book about malls because I thought it would be funny. A self-deprecating poke at the self-deprecating place I've come from, a reprieve from the more serious issues that terrify me and make me question if it's worth doing anything at all.

I found something that looks a lot different from what I set out to find. I found that the history of the mall is a mirror. The things that have happened here reflect and magnify the conditions that have built it. And I found myself reflected back to me, a glimpse of what it might mean to become a person in the same time and place. In this very weird, often bad place, I also found clues about how another life is possible.

So, I can't look away from the mall. And I don't think that we should. For better or worse, malls are signs of our lives, and West Edmonton Mall is confirmation of mine.

Space

Before it was West Edmonton Mall, it was a field outside the limits of Edmonton – a city named for another place, the English hometown of one of its colonizers. In Cree, the land is called amiskwaciy-wâskahikan, which translates into 'Beaver Hills House.' The river seven kilometres south of the mall has long been a place to meet and trade.

Today, West Edmonton Mall rises like a spray of brutalist mountains from Anthony Henday Drive, a ring-road moat dividing the city from an ever-expanding sprawl of housing developments. The mall spans nearly fifty city blocks and is bordered by the world's largest parking lot. You can't get a photo that captures its size. It's an amorphous puzzle of material, defying faithful description, facing inwardly on itself, shy. You cannot see inside the mall unless you are inside the mall. And when you're inside the mall, there's no indication that you're in Edmonton, a real place on a map, and not an unbounded state of escalators, H&Ms, and food courts. The mall becomes tethered to a place with a name only if you thumb through your own memories of the place and trace them to a feeling of home. And so in this mall, as in all malls, I have already seen everything I could possibly buy for the rest of my life. Here's Uniqlo, here's Urban Outfitters. Here I am, straight-up turned on by the smell of Auntie Anne's pretzels. Thanks to globalization, I get to experience this sensation around the world.

———

The aura of elsewhere permeates the world's most-visited malls. In Dubai, the Mall of the Emirates whisks you out of the dry heat and onto an indoor ski slope. A mall in Qatar is explicitly modelled on the Grand Canal Shoppes at the Venetian resort in Las Vegas – not the real Venetian canals in Italy. Dizzyingly, the replicated indoor gondolas and starry-night ceiling in Qatar are geographically closer to the real Venice than they are to the simulations on the Strip. Another mall simulation is run by Caesars in Atlantic City. Here, you can sit on Adirondack chairs in an indoor shallow pit of sand, in front of a wall of windows. If you turn around, there's a recreation of the Atlantic City pier behind you. If you turn back around, the real, much bigger, pier presents itself to you underneath your nose outdoors.

I find this nowhereness virtuous, like an homage to malls' original design, which has been essentially preserved since the prototype – which in turn was born of transcontinental inspiration. And even the most basic mall qualifies as an escape if it's slightly hotter or cooler than the temperature outside. Most have nothing to do with the actual landscape they're built upon; there's no such thing as a mall that hasn't been inspired by another. Now, Southdale Center has renovated itself enough times that the first-ever mall no longer looks like itself.

Shopping in other places is disappointing after you've grown up in Edmonton. West Edmonton Mall has made an obsession out of the simulacra – you're never completely convinced that you've left Edmonton, but the effort to dazzle you screams from each of its fantasy-stirring features. The indoor waterpark adorns itself with a fake beach and palm trees. Nearby, a lagoon twists through the main floor, housing a replica of Christopher Columbus's *Santa María* and a tank where sea lions perform elaborate routines to pop music. Another section of the mall, called Europa Boulevard, intentionally resembles a European high street. Its actual resemblance to anything beyond Alberta is questionable, but the quaint Juliet balcony facade lends streetwear stores an elevated *je ne sais quoi*. There's also Bourbon Street, where giant Mardi Gras masks once welcomed diners to Hooters and similar restaurants. Life-size models of cabs and drunk men, even sex workers being arrested by cops, rounded out the theme. The strip is now stylized as BRBN st., sanitized of vowels and the Mardi Gras theme of yore. There's the Fantasyland Hotel, which still inexplicably offers rooms in African and Polynesian themes. In 2007, World Vision opened an interactive village near the HMV where you could cosplay as a disadvantaged teenage mother if you had time to kill before heading to the parking lot.

When the third phase of West Edmonton Mall, which included the submarines and dolphin tanks, opened in 1985, Nader Ghermezian boldly declared that nobody in the western hemisphere would have to travel to Europe anymore: 'When you come to West Edmonton Mall, it's a world by itself – a world within a world.' The statement in itself sounds bizarre, especially to anyone from Canada. Edmonton, especially in the 1980s, could not be remotely worldly, let alone meaningfully distinct from any other city in Western Canada. In reality, however, Ghermezian's vision did put Edmonton on the map. Whether Edmonton likes to admit it or not, many people only know it for its big, otherworldly mall. West Edmonton Mall attracts more than thirty million visitors a year – roughly twice as many as Disneyland.

———

Malls are among the spaces cultural anthropologist Marc Augé discusses in his 1992 book, *Non-Places: Introduction to an Anthropology of Supermodernity*. He defines the non-place in contrast to sociological or anthropological place, the environments where people authentically commune with one another and, as a result, form distinct cultures and selfhoods. These places have traditionally been an anthropologist's touch point into crafting a particular understanding of what it means to be a human being. Non-places, on the other hand, are the big, anonymous, transient spaces one moves through without forming meaningful social bonds or identity or engaging with history: huge highways, airports, and hotel lobbies, the incomprehensibly loose space of a conference centre. One's point of entry and exit to the mortal plane likely happens in the non-space of a hospital, surrounded by fewer family members than strangers.

This sense of placelessness has only proliferated in the thirty years since Augé put a name to it. Now, the line between places and non-places is blurry. It seems quaint, for example, to remember a time when travelling to a new city offered a truly novel experience. Once, staying in an Airbnb felt like stepping into a stranger's life. The first one I ever stayed at was in South Side Chicago. The host left after giving my partner and me a quick tour through the place, but I felt his presence, even uncomfortably so, throughout our stay. His son's crib was nestled against the bed we slept in; photos of this baby were hung on the wall and watched us do everything. Unfamiliar hair stuck to the bathtub. And somehow, this intimacy was less creepy than its near-total absence from every vacation rental I have stayed at in recent memory: the deadbolted mystery closets and basements, a beige eternity of Live Laugh Love screenprints, and gigantic fridges home only to the carton of milk the previous guest didn't have time to finish. The avatars of the host and me communicate in a tightly choreographed ritual to maintain our mutual five-star ratings; I pick the correct number of exclamation marks to convey my delight in stripping my bedsheets, taking out the recycling, and leaving without a trace at 11:00 a.m. And when I leave the Airbnb, I go to a coffee shop and a brewery that are identical to the ones I like in Vancouver, which are identical to the ones I like in Edmonton.

Does a craft brewery enhance a city's local charm any more than a Starbucks, when the next one over is churning out the same permeation of hazy IPAs served by identical tattooed men? The aesthetic, the beer, the men: I'm attracted to all of them. It's not a bad thing; I can find things I like no matter where I go. The planet follows me everywhere.

What I know for certain is that malls are the most non-placey places imaginable. Inside them, we feel the totality of the world without meaningfully comprehending or impressing upon it. Like, the *worldliness* of a mall is immense. I can't possibly wrap my mind around the origin of each of the articles of clothing circulating through the mall, each made by a person I will never meet in a country I will never see for myself. I see literally thousands of people. I even accidentally brush against some of them among the sales racks and breathe air that has passed through their own bodies. But I don't know them (I don't have any interest in knowing them) and they won't know me. We transcend – or repress – the real parts of ourselves when we assume the shared identity of shoppers. And this is all so normal to the extent that I feel high trying to articulate it as an arrangement, this freaky way we arrange ourselves. Conceptually, I understand that things have only been this way for such a short time. I have no understanding of what the time before this would have felt like; I don't yearn to know it, either.

To be honest, I enjoy how the harsher parts of myself flatten when I shop in a mall. After being there for an hour or so, I feel like I'm in a vacuum and the only way out is through shopping. Then I shift into the mentally liberating and financially devastating fuck-it point of no return, where I begin spending money like it isn't real, because I no longer seem like a real person. Suddenly I'm reciting my email for a newsletter I'll never read in exchange for 15 per cent off my purchase, which feels more like a transactional pleasantry than anything. I'm paying on credit, which means my jeans cost little more than moving a couple more numbers around the next time I muster the courage to open my banking app. I prefer this charade over buying things online, which I've internalized as a less moral cop-out, as if a certain type of shopping can feel *too* late-capitalist. There's no drama or labour in clicking a button! Using my real body to shop, on the other hand, is a true experience. While wrangling my mortal form into a pair of jeans I saw a teenager wear on TikTok, I'm combatting not only physics but my own ancient problem of never recognizing myself in change-room mirrors. The Aritzia saleswoman who mercilessly insists I go down a size, even though we both know it isn't remotely possible, is following her own script handed to her by the elusive echelons of management. But that hardly matters to me. This whole act might be the most I exert myself some Saturdays.

The dissociative compulsion we feel when shopping is known as the 'Gruen transfer,' named after Victor, the godfather of the modern mall. More than anyone else, Gruen is responsible for establishing the mall as a true portal of retail, an environment that primes us to want things we may not have wanted before. The first interior shopping experience of its kind, Southdale Center's two 'anchor' department stores functioned as magnetic poles, coaxing shoppers past the smaller stores on their way to the main attractions, a structural feature we see in most malls today. Another effect of Gruen's influence: malls are islands. Developers still intentionally build malls away from other business hubs to isolate them from more attractive shopping locations. We're unlikely, as a result, to leave the mall to check out other options. Unsurprisingly, people tend to spend more money when they're shopping in person; at least 50 per cent of purchases at the mall are unplanned. Speaking for myself, I believe that the specific mall I am visiting will provide whatever I'm looking for that day. Like destiny.

Considered under these terms, shopping at a mall feels less like an autonomous choice and more like submitting to a higher power. That helps explain the popular rhetorical, if not effective, ire against malls. In Costa Mesa, California, a shopping centre absorbs this affect into its name: the Anti-Mall. To use its own words, the Anti-Mall is 'the only progressive, lifestyle-culture, specialty retail shopping destination in Orange County,' offering vegan doughnuts and locally designed clothing (and an Urban Outfitters) in a breezy, Insta-grammable outdoor venue. More often, the cultural cachet of hating the mall is shorthanded in language. We use *mall* as an adjective to denote a baser, mass-approved version of teenagers (rats), food, or music. To *mallify* something is to turn a more pure social space, like a neighbourhood or a monument, into a banal site of consumption.

When I was a teenager, a friend or two would spontaneously declare that they *hated* the mall; I started saying the same, although it didn't entirely make sense to me – forming an opinion against anything, however, was thrilling. I don't think I hate the mall now, but I have allegiance to the handful of people who tweet 'I hate the mall' every day, one of the purest expressions you can make on the internet, rattled off while taking a breather in a bathroom stall or feeling hypoglycemic in line for the change room, nobody else around to witness your exasperation. Saying that you hate the mall is like clawing a breathing hole through a plastic bag that's been placed over your head; if the mall represents a collapse of psychology and aesthetic, you can assert yourself as an individual through creating an explicit distance of your own.

Theorists have conceptualized the Bad Mall Feeling in various shades of chagrin, none more pointedly than Dutch architect Rem Koolhaas. In his 2001 essay 'Junkspace' – stretching across seventeen pages in a single, unbroken paragraph, riddled with ellipses and acerbic metaphor – Koolhaas condemns megastructures such as airports, open-concept offices, and of course malls, the seemingly endless, ever-expanding interior spaces enabled by air conditioning and buttressed by Muzak. The form of these spaces reflects their function: invented only for the un-creative, un-individual human avatars of economies. Junkspace is the detritus of modernity, Koolhaas writes. 'It makes you uncertain where you are, obscures where you go, undoes where you were.'

Marc Augé, on the other hand, didn't write *Non-Places* to condemn such spaces. (Which, given their dominance over our lives, seems like it would be as reasonable as condemning the existence of animals, the sky, or time.) His conception of non-places is value-neutral. In fact, he mentions that, for some, a real sense of place can exist in the non-place – every non-place is a real place for someone. The cashier working at the store we bought our jeans from doesn't just pass through the mall. The structure will remain a monolith of her memory years from now, when she reflects on the summer she spent working at Zara between graduating high school and going to university. Her boss wore one of those headsets and was a power-tripping dick, but she met her first boyfriend in line at Freshii; she dumped him while they sat in his car in the parking lot, in front of what used to be the

Zellers entrance. In the future, she will feel as nostalgic for the bad air conditioning and harsh lighting as for any other formative aspect of her life's story. This also translates into the attachment we might feel to global brands in the non-place. If you love McDonald's – especially if you have intimate memories attached to McDonald's – seeing the golden arches in a foreign land can make the more unfamiliar place feel like home.

Augé, then, isn't trying to moralize these spaces. Instead, he's highlighting a momentous shift in human livelihoods and, importantly, the need to study them differently. The anthropological traditions of studying now-dated 'modern' lives can hardly parse the pronounced individuality and dissociation of our current ones. Specifically, supermodernity explodes the field's interest in social culture. For the first time, people are experiencing the definitive moments of their lives alone. At the end of the book, Augé calls for a new field of study in itself: 'an ethnology of solitude.'

This perspective resonates with me – so much of my life has happened in my own head. I need to have an idea fully formed before I even consider mentioning it to someone else; as a kid, I would go whole summers without seeing kids who weren't my cousins or siblings, for no reason except that I just never asked people to hang out. I wonder if this has something to do with my built environment. Looking at my coming of age from a bird's-eye view would show the small dot of me gliding between different big containers: my bedroom, a car, my school, the mall. This could explain who I am, as if these spaces compressed me deeper into myself. But then, of course, everyone else I know moved through identical containers, and I don't think it's had the same effect on all of us. I can only hope that the same compression has happened to them, too, and they just don't talk about it, that I'm not a complete alien for being this way, that the thread of loneliness runs through most of us.

I didn't hate growing up in this landscape. I guess I didn't know otherwise; on a larger scale, these huge spaces imbued my life with profundity. In the summer, my two siblings and I spent our days between our grandma's house and the back of my dad's Ford Focus as he drove around the city with one hand, taking business calls on his flip phone in the other. Sometimes, we would get to the mall before any of the stores had opened, eat cinnamon buns, and peer through the gate at the frozen roller coasters. Those mornings, it felt like the mall was all ours – I would pretend that we were either millionaires or royalty and that all of this was our castle. I always wanted to stay longer than we did, not to shop but just to sit still and spend a bit more time in my imagination. I hated the cold slapping my face when we walked out of the building and the shock of frozen seat-belt metal biting the skin beneath my T-shirt. And although I wish I wasn't like this, I hated the warm body of my sister, always in the middle seat, resting her head on my shoulder when she fell asleep between my brother and me.

I did like the sitting, the thinking, and the music, though. Instead of the radio, my dad cycled through a tightly curated rotation of rock CDs. I spent a lot of time looking out the car window onto Edmonton, thinking dramatic thoughts to *The Best Beer Drinking Album in the World … Ever!* I was too young to understand what a closing time was and why someone would write an emotional song about it, but something resonated about wanting to be taken home.

There was a period of my life when I wanted nothing but the experience of Junk- and non-places. My first urban experience was walking Main Street, U.S.A., in Disneyland. I felt nationalistic, strangers smiling at each other as we watched fireworks soundtracked by anthems we all knew. I spent my days in windowless schools, and I grew up in a warm, comfortable home surrounded by other warm, comfortable homes, where it would take ten minutes to drive to a friend's house or any store. Walking anywhere was an occasion. I dreamed of buying a McMansion on a dirt plot. Having my birthday parties at the biggest mall seemed as normal as riding the yellow bus to school.

I'm not sure when this changed. Having friends who increasingly spoke about wanting to leave must have played a role. It would take a long time before I would ever come up with a good reason to leave a place that had everything I needed as long as I could borrow my parents' car to get to it. Every time I try to articulate why I left, I come across incorrectly, sounding either irrational for intentionally leaving somewhere that makes life easy to live or like I'm insulting someone who finds meaning in a place where I will never live again.

These Junk- and non-places are woven into every part of me. As a result, I'm not sure I can truly ever fully understand their critique. It's also hard to be critical of these places without feeling like I'm betraying my essence. I even feel offensive writing this down.

Koolhaas, writing in *Harvard Design School Guide to Shopping*, was speaking to a receptive audience: people already primed to identify with a suspicion toward the buildings – and culture – of the mainstream. I, on the other hand, had to google 'what is architecture' to understand Koolhaas's point. (This is what I learned: if we take our definition from Vitruvius, architecture is the 'artful arrangement of durable and functional spaces that stimulate the senses.') Hearing a takedown of the buildings where I spend most of my time inspires my mind to escape to the same place I go whenever someone begins telling the unfortunate tale of their parents selling the beloved summer cabin or their NFT losing value. I touch my phone, take flight to somewhere of more personal attachment. I was never invested in the value of that place or thing; I cannot feel its loss in the same way. Even Koolhaas admits Junkspace emerged as punishment for architects' inability to talk about space in a straightforward way. If someone could just accessibly make the case for better space, even the uneducated, the blatantly capitalist, would have stakes in doing something about the kind we've got.

I'm not sure what I, as a non-architect, can do with this perspective, beyond becoming newly aware that I have no personal history predating Junkspace. This means I, and most people I know, take for granted a landscape that scholars like Augé and Koolhaas have identified in the negative. At one point in my life, I wouldn't have been able to envision an alternative. An entire style of life that's indefensible to some is, for many others, as real as it will ever get; I can only pretend to be nostalgic for this place that predates my own reality. Realistically, I don't believe Augé and Koolhaas would have intended me to read their writing at all.

When I first saw Vikky Alexander's work at the Vancouver Art Gallery, I thought I was looking at a wall of collages: slick strips of magazine photos arranged to form a prism of contemporary North American life. Lots of chrome and brass surfaces, people walking aimlessly in a crowd, a lottery ticket booth, a palm tree, and an ocean – a slice of an ad for a Caribbean vacation. Walking closer, I realized the 'collages' were unadulterated 35 mm photographs of West Edmonton Mall in the late eighties; the mirrors panelling every vertical surface of the mall lend this effect, fracturing the gaze of the shoppers inside and the viewer outside the photo. The vacation advertisement is just the blue waves of the World Waterpark; the 'clipping' foregrounding it is the bulk-candy store. While staring straight ahead, you can see the disparate chaos in the three distinct levels of the mall, both beyond and behind Alexander's vantage point, the way holding a mirror to another mirror reflects yourself into infinity.

Alexander has since documented other hotbeds of simulacrum and tourism, including Las Vegas and Disneyland. Capturing the positive feeling in such places can be as difficult as taking a good picture of the moon with an iPhone; Alexander's work exposes the constructed nature of these places, but her photographs aren't pedantic. The beach looks fake, and I still want to visit it; the animal-shaped hedges and the boat ferrying tourists in her shots of the It's a Small World ride clearly represent manufactured entertainment on a massive scale without dulling the warm invitation of a vacation.

Alexander's work is refreshing in contrast to other contemporary art that engages with the allure of our built environment, like *Dismaland*, Banksy's satirical pop-up theme park, which included pieces like an oil-caliphate-themed minigolf course and a crashed Cinderella pumpkin swarmed by paparazzi; one of the only souvenirs you could buy was a balloon with the words 'I'M AN IMBECILE' scrawled across it, all a glaring commentary on the fact that we really do *live in a society*, and that – rats! – there is most definitely no ethical consumption under capitalism.

Alexander's photographs don't make me feel like a complete loser for having my genuine desires, which include dipping my feet into the glassy waters of the World Water-park. During the early, isolated days of the COVID-19 pandemic, this desire contorted into the fantasy of filling a huge cup with water from the wave pool and drinking it in a single gulp. I also wouldn't mind riding the tallest waterslide completely naked. For me, the draw of any amusement park is less a yearning for adrenaline and more a yearning to submit to a higher power. I enjoy feeling held in place by a series of mechanical devices all built for my entertainment. Bring me to the edge of danger, sweep me away from danger.

In other words, a desire to escape isn't a desire for nothingness – it's a desire to feel something different. The experience of time and space in these non-places is still real as anything. For example, we don't forget where we are when we visit a simulated space. I don't cower in fear of the world's largest duck in Andrew, Alberta. The people peering down onto the Atlantic City boardwalk likely find nothing disturb-ing about sitting in its simulacrum. The fake boardwalk must make the real one seem more important. We are conscious of our modernity.

This shift does, however, represent our current postmodern – or, in other words, the 'nothing is authentic, but it doesn't matter' – era of tourism. People who theorize about contemporary tourism speak about an 'aesthetic enjoyment of surfaces' being the true motivator and pleasure of travelling. We can find something authentic based on our belief alone without needing any proof of how genuine it is: just ask a Disney adult about the true magic they experience while hugging an overheating college student in a cartoon mouse costume.

Any recent gestures toward authenticity in travel, anyway, are likely to be manufactured. Think of the painstaking efforts taken to restore and maintain historical sites: the millions of dollars the Italian government is spending to redo the floors of the Colosseum, for example. When we look at a da Vinci painting in the Louvre, we're looking not at a 'raw' painting but at the product of subtle touch-ups and cleanings performed by museum staff over the centuries. The settler public is now gaining a clearer awareness of how even national parks, often depicted as the purest form of escape, only gained their 'untouched' allure through the systematic removal of Indigenous people.

We all drift between experiences of realness and unrealness, tricked by fake details, untrusting of real details, attaching real emotion and feeling to details of either description. Academics have also described something called 'heritage flow,' the sublimity of losing oneself in the immensity of time. This has been documented in modern-day tourists encountering ancient architectural sites, but I wonder if it could be applied to malls as well, specifically the wave pool in the World Waterpark. The pool sits still before an air horn signals that the waves are going to start. Hearing the horn and the screams echoing off the immense dome of the park, I have always felt like I'm a small creature participating in something vast and ancient.

Alexander captures the truth of this experience in her photography. Her observant eye, however, isn't meant to be a balm for whatever odd feelings accompany our enjoyment of the mall. Instead, her work reveals the real, kind-of-cursed seduction of Disneyland and Disneyland-inspired environments as a manifestation of our culture's desires. The result is an image that looks attractive, but a bit wrong. Similarly, her earlier work superimposes images of beautiful female models over postcards of pristine mountain ranges. Both the woman and the landscape look good. You want to touch the woman; you want to book a nice trip. By holding the images in balance with each other and blowing them up, though, Alexander also attunes us to the calculative gaze of advertorial photography, the apparatus of our desire – what turns us on isn't necessarily pure. Being recognized in this way is both validating and off-putting; you're yanked in before having the mirror held under your face at an unflattering angle. Alexander's work, then, zeroes in on the inevitable dysfunction of utopia. Even though we have infinite capital and resources to build precisely what we want, the dream doesn't look right when it comes to life.

'I think utopias are inherently flawed, they can't exist,' Alexander once said in an interview with the National Gallery of Canada. 'The minute you get it, it's normal life and it's not ideal anymore. It's only ideal in the possibility.'

This checks out. My fantasy of being liberated by visiting the waterpark, for example, is best explored in the contours of my own sicko mind. When I go there for real, I'm assailed by the sounds of screaming kids echoing off a million walls and plastic surfaces. I see a lot of floating Band-Aids. I can't hear myself think, and I inevitably miss the fantasy's purity when it lived in my brain. This happens all the time. I go to Vegas, I complain the whole time I'm there; after I leave I dream of going back and getting an even bigger margarita.

————

We get the word *utopia* from a book written by Thomas More, a sixteenth-century Catholic philosopher. *Utopia* is a homophone of the Greek word for 'no place,' which sounds exactly the same as 'good place.' It's a cool fact and a sweet rhetorical Easter egg for conservative politicians: we should be pragmatic and tax people less because the socialist good place doesn't exist. Dreams aren't real, you guys! I have more fun thinking about More's wordplay evoking the incomprehensibility of a dream, both the kind we have as individuals and the kind we have as a collective. I feel insane when trying to explain what happened to me while I was sleeping. Dreams become strange the moment we know they're dreams; if only I could get it down on paper, I could be known a little more truly by the people around me.

The features of our utopias are directly informed by our present material conditions. Cockaigne, an imaginary place often featured in medieval poetry, is now understood as a peasant's daydream: rivers flow with honey and wine, there's no animal shit to shovel, and the livestock walk around pre-seasoned, presenting you with a knife to slice them. Our contemporary values surrounding labour have also constrained our cultural imagination of utopia. As a kid, I dreamed about the indulgence of the Emerald City and Willy Wonka's factory. I desperately wanted to pet the colour-changing horse, be pampered by three different workers in matching green outfits, dive into a river of chocolate. I usually stopped the movies early because I hated the endings. Charlie only inherits the all-providing factory because he's more virtuous than the greedy rich kids.

That never sat right with me. Who among us wouldn't break an odd man's rules to try the cool gum? And the Emerald City is only a product of a megalomaniac who in turn is just a character in a dream; Dorothy has to go home to Kansas and realizes, to my disappointment, that there's no place like it. Even the hedonistic paradise of Cockaigne was something to be earned – peasants had to wade through neck-high pig shit for seven years to reach it. Although some read it as a defiant satire on the asceticism expected of medieval peasants, the myth of Cockaigne has been more popularly reappropriated as a moralizing tale: true indulgence comes only to those who've earned it.

Walt Disney had a similar rationale for his own attempt at utopia. His original vision for the Epcot park didn't involve drinking your way around the small world of eleven different cultural pavilions; the park was to be an urban community outfitted with the best that modern technology had to offer.

The company took his plans in a different direction after Disney's death, but he made his intentions explicit while he was alive: 'There will be no retirees,' he wrote plainly. 'Everyone must be employed.'

Lately, I have become obsessed with watching vlogs made by employees of the Disney College Program – Disney-obsessed students documenting their experiences of making minimum wage working in the parks. Nearly all of them cry when they get their positions, and nearly all of them cry when they're working nine days in a row painting bratty American faces. I'm fascinated by how the fantasy of a brand clashes with the material conditions of being a worker. But I would be lying if I expressed complete cynicism about this. I love the mindless escape of watching these young people work at a place that's exploiting them and nevertheless experience awe while eating a plant-based bratwurst at a *Toy Story*–themed restaurant. It's like they've figured out something I haven't. Whatever it is, I hover as close as I can, watching them as I eat my own dinner alone on my couch.

If you just look at the potential of the space alone – the sheer amount of luxury vaulted inside of it – the mall could be a pretty perfect place: protecting us from the elements, entertaining us, giving us everything we need to make ourselves more beautiful. Walter Benjamin, in his analysis of the early precursors to shopping malls, refers to Western European arcades as 'dream-houses of the collective' teasing us with a certain heaven of endless treats, so close that they're basically ours. Some retail developers even say it outright. The Ghermezians' newest mall is elegantly called American Dream. It was originally named Xanadu, and the

Ghermezians' company, Triple Five Group, took over the project after the first and second owners went bankrupt. Across the Hudson and Hackensack Rivers from Manhattan, American Dream is the second-largest mall in the U.S., after the Mall of America. Its waterpark is nearly identical to the one in West Edmonton Mall, except it's sponsored by DreamWorks – a biblically large inflatable Shrek lords over the wave pool, which really does sound like heaven to me. There's another Xanadú mall in Madrid, a Utopia City mall in Mumbai, and a Utopia mall in Sweden. Google Reviews users report that the Swedish Utopia has an above-average food court but the stores don't always have what the reviewers are looking for.

Marketing a mall as a dream come true is pretty ghoulish, ironic at best. Of course, the mall is utopia for the people developing it, a means to the end of making a shit-ton of money. For those of us shopping there, it will never reach that platonic ideal of meeting all our needs and desires. For one, it can't provide everything we want and need because we don't have infinite money. And the mall is not constantly available to us – it closes every night, and we have to go home. It might even be the one place where we can have the urban-adjacent experience of walking in a crowd without seeing people who are homeless. Mall security can look at anyone using the mall incorrectly, call it loitering, and escort them from the utopia. A mall is a dream in the same way our brains chew up and spit out the random stuff from our day while we're sleeping. It's a way to make sense of where we've come from, but it's not our place to belong. So, if the mall is a real-ization of the subconscious, it's an imperfect one – unless the collective unconscious features more capital and subjugation than I'm currently giving it credit for.

But the reverse isn't true: the mall appears perfectly in my dreams. According to www.dreaminterp.com, dreaming about the mall means 'those things that you need (affection, friendship, spiritual support, quality time with people you care about) are available to you … However,' the site warns, 'you may need to learn exactly where to look, how to select what you need, and how to ask for these things when you need them.'

I have had good and bad dreams about the mall, some mundane and some profound. The only time I have seen people after they've died has been in my dreams. Sometimes it takes place in my unconscious mind's reinvention of West Edmonton Mall, where we walk the long, bright stretches of stores together. I can mentally trace the whole geography of the mall, and sometimes, if I have trouble sleeping, I picture myself walking from one end to the other, until I drift off. It's like how, when I press my fingers into my eyelids, I still see the pattern from my parents' first couch – I know we're all probably seeing the same stars flashing from our retinas, but I can't stop seeing the places I've been, even when my eyes are closed.

Recently, my friend told me about how she took shrooms in an old-growth forest on Vancouver Island. Lying on the forest floor, gazing at the awe-inspiring, all-knowing canopy above her, she exclaimed that it looked like Galaxyland.

———

Living in proximity to a spectacle is like having your brain infected with a riddle. I could spend a lifetime learning about this mall and still not completely understand it. West Edmonton Mall's sheer size and the fact it has impressed itself upon millions of people means I will never capture it perfectly – it has as many sides to consider as a sphere. When I think about West Edmonton Mall, I have empathy for people who won't shut up about being from Toronto or New York. How can you ever stop talking about a place where so many things happen? Every time we talk about where we're from, we get closer to figuring out what it all meant. But we get farther, too – each new detail we learn clouds out a possible answer.

It would be sweet to feel at home in a city that's so large and daunting to tourists – to have textured memories beyond an abstract locus of Business and Opportunity. I feel a bit of this stupid pride now living in Vancouver, as if the urban tangle is something I've outsmarted, having a favourite beach spot nobody else knows about and navigating the bus routes from memory. The experience of growing up near an otherworldly tourist destination hits different, though. You became familiar with a place that's intentionally abstracted from reality. Or, more accurately, the search for familiarity is never complete.

Evan Prosofsky, a cinematographer who grew up in Edmonton, never got used to the unreality of the mall: the flamingos, the submarines, the roller coasters. In interviews, he has explained that the enclosed waterpark gave him a futuristic, apocalyptic vibe – as if it were the last beach on earth, preserved for the aliens or the wealthy under a protective glass canopy.

Prosofsky released a sixteen-minute experimental film, *Waterpark*, in 2013. It opens with punchy archival shots of young men surfing in the wave pool in the eighties, overlaid with the booming voice of advertisements for the mall: 'You never have to paddle out to the break, you never have to wait for a wave – these guys think it's great.' Then, an increasingly eerie, droning score fades over the cheerful surf rock as the film cuts to stark shots of the Edmonton river valley in early spring or late autumn. The saturation from the mall's interior drains and the real landscape looks grey by comparison. The camera then brings us back to safety, the mall, where we catch quick glances of its various unrealities – Bourbon Street, a minigolf course, the amusement park, the *Santa Maria*, sea lions, and penguins – before spending the remaining thirteen minutes sinking into the waterpark.

The waterpark, rendered by Prosofsky, becomes an uncompromisingly physical space. A group of tween girls sit and self-consciously readjust their bikinis. Bodies are hurled around in the surf, forming a slow-moving animal of its own. The whole time, people peer into the wave pool from the observation deck above. The colours, the bathing suits, the relaxation on people's faces make the wave pool feel convincingly tropical. But Prosofsky doesn't let us settle into the fantasy; we see the grand, seemingly impossible apparatuses upholding the waterslides: the beams suspending them in the air, and then the glass-and-metal canopy lording over the 'beach' and 'ocean' below it. A chasm furrows between the soft bodies and hard, inorganic structure. In the final segment, a man hurls himself off the tall tower at the mouth of the pool, as if he were flying or doing something much worse, but he is, of course, tethered by a thick red bungee cord. He's not going anywhere.

Prosofsky illustrates the feeling I have been struggling to name, to be small at the feet of a physical and historical mechanism inconceivably larger than me, negotiating my thoughts very privately despite being surrounded by thousands of people, each vibrating with their own complicated inner life.

The New Pornographers' 'Whiteout Conditions' music video represents three of those visitors as a closeted oil rig worker, a man who killed someone in a car accident, and a woman who's hired a male escort, all separately seeking escapism at West Edmonton Mall. None of them gets the release they're looking for. The environment only acts as a pressure cooker for their inner turmoil as they get drunk in their respective themed-hotel-room hot tubs, fuck strangers, and fling themselves into the sea of bodies in the wave pool. By the end of the music video, they're all drowning in a black substance. Is it oil? I don't know. Oil, which is driven by and drives materialism, which is abstracting people from their true desires, and also killing the environment and all of us. It's all a bit on the nose but locates the mall as a place that both manifests desire and snatches it away, leaving the visitors with various spots on their hands that they can't seem to wash off.

The song throbs with the urgent self-importance of the alt-rock music that defined my adolescence – Arcade Fire, Death Cab, Stars, the Killers; they served as my morning alarm and my soundtrack to driving around St. Albert. They're self-contained spectacles, overanalyzing grocery stores and suburban cul-de-sacs as if they were passages in an AP English exam, before cascading into dramatic orchestral choruses professing the angst of being somewhere but longing to go somewhere else.

The movements of this dramatic modern rock mirrored my own particular landscape of unbearable winters and sudden hot summers, the flat expanses of fields punctuated by shocks of sublime infrastructure. I could never wrap my head around ring roads, how small I was and how fast we were going. The songs sound climactic, as in: the ending is coming soon.

———

I do wonder how Koolhaas would write about the typical North American childhood, if there's agency any of us can find within a space through imprinting upon it. I wonder if I would have imagined more radical possibility or even sociality for my life if my surroundings looked different – but I also can't imagine anything that could teem with more people or possibility than this mall.

Koolhaas's angst probably has nothing to do with me or anyone other than Koolhaas. In the last passage of the Junkspace essay, Koolhaas reveals his hand: 'Will Junkspace invade the body? Through the vibes of the cell phone? Has it already? Through Botox injections? Collagen? Silicone implants? Liposuction? Penis enlargements? Does gene therapy announce a total reengineering according to Junkspace? Is each of us a mini-construction site? Is mankind the sum of three to five billion individual upgrades? Is it a repertoire of reconfiguration that facilitates the intromission of a new species into its self-made Junksphere? The cosmetic is cosmic … '

He ends his essay on this ellipsis, as if the trail of thought will never end. To me, this exposes the root of his distaste for supermodern space, nothing much to do with architecture or even the alienating labour relations of late capitalism. It's less criticism than it is a bare fear that modernity will spiral out of control and into our own bodies, then into the more impossible-to-answer questions: What then? When does the body end and machine begin? It's a bit funny to read a presumably able-bodied man, in the year 2001, forecast the modifiable body as a terrifying future prospect. (My Botox says hi!) He does capture, however, the terror of finding ourselves in an infinite environment, of our lives taking shape in spaces that have expanded beyond our comprehension. That's the scary thing, not being able to grasp it all. What if we've gone too far to come back?

I do empathize with Koolhaas's ideas – I've felt some strain of this acutely on my own. Despite the progressiveness I want to project about myself, my first reaction to any change is an immediate longing for things to stay the same. Some shade of this tipped toward agoraphobia during the first year of the COVID-19 pandemic. I can't find a better phrase for it than 'an irrational hatred of the built environment.' I loathed bridges, airplanes, cars, boats, young trees planted in the sidewalk that would eventually become too big, tear up the sidewalk with their roots, then be torn down and shredded by the city. During the first pandemic summer, I drove onto a ferry and felt like I was being eaten twice: first by the metal of the car, and second by the jaws of the boat. The sky was orange with forest-fire smoke drifting from south of the border. We've fucked up, I'd think to myself. The only way we can find something that resembles satisfaction on this finite planet is by pretending that we're infinite; that's why the earth is burning. And then I'd think, no, fuck you – I didn't do anything wrong, like, I was literally just born.

I was convinced that we were living in the end times, and while I didn't think anyone deserved to be subjected to that, I felt particularly slighted that I had to experience it. Everything felt like a consequence of human selfishness and of modernity – something unquestionably of myself but completely outside of my control. I have been made by and have made an inherently destructive force. And there was nothing I could do to escape it. I couldn't walk in the woods without travelling down a road that cut the forest in half.

Everything about my life felt more fake than ever before. The fact that I grew up in a place founded on stolen land and petrochemicals, the fact that the only way I knew to make myself feel better was to buy things online, which never actually satisfied me and made me feel worse when the package appeared at my door. I was obviously privileged to be feeling these things but was also becoming unconvinced that my situation, let alone other people's, was real. The most useful thing I figured I could do was to trap myself in my apartment, occasionally taking little quarantine walks with a rotten feeling inside my body. I did stop being like this, eventually, although a more quiet version of this narrative sometimes whirrs in the background on days when I'm feeling bleak about where everything is heading. I can't remember the day I stopped being like this. I know it got better when I started seeing people again. Really, I think it was all happening because I was alone.

Youth

First, they take their shirts off. Then, the boys throw themselves over the brass railing, plunging two levels – the height of the Cinnabon sign – into the mall water, narrowly missing the fake rocks and real, hard floor.

On YouTube, it's basically become a genre of its own: young men jumping into West Edmonton Mall's Deep Sea Lagoon, home of the *Santa Maria* replica. Some wear tight Speedos as if they're training for an Olympic high dive. Others, uncomfortably, are wearing jeans. One guy jumps off the railing with his skateboard pressed beneath his feet, making the sickest half-pipe out of the air itself. In most of them, the boy holding the camera shrieks to himself (*no fuckin' way, no fuckin' way!*) in the hysterical girly squeal a young man makes only in the presence of other guys, rapt in the act of something outrageous.

I can never look away from a guy doing stupid shit. I'm easily ensnared by hockey-fight and ski-stunt compilations in a way that must be biological. Watching young men dive through the mall is particularly striking, even more than seeing them jump off a cliff or a half-pipe. For one, these guys are using the mall all wrong. They're turning it into something different, perverting this self-contained, vanilla leisure enclosure into a death trap. Then they flip that death trap the bird, to the delight of all these friends who love them. I love how time slows as the guy falls through the sky, this graceful vulnerability and trust that the water will catch him. And it almost always does; I've only seen one video where a boy fell through the flimsy roof of the Cinnabon, but he wasn't aiming for the water, anyway.

In some ways, my gaze is protective. As long as I'm looking, my superstition goes, nothing bad can happen. Or if he hits his head and needs me to call for help, my virtual presence seems like it could still be useful. But in a bigger way, seeing men throw themselves off buildings stirs envy, and later frustration, inside me. Like, here he is with all this youth and agility and future, ready to piss it away between his skull and a concrete surface. I wonder what it would feel like to not be afraid, who I would be if fear meant something different. I don't think I would be the one to leap over the mall railing, but I bet it would improve my life dramatically enough that I cannot begin to define it now.

———

Teenagers are archetypically beheld in awe or abjection: either an unnuanced, asexual embodiment of virtue itself – Malala, Greta – or they're vaping, they're ruining culture, never not texting or TikTokking or whatever it is now. They won't stay off my lawn! (I don't have one, but you know what I mean.) The word *ephebiphobia* refers to an extreme fear of teenagers – it also signals that the concept of young people scaring the living shit out of adults is felt psychologically and culturally enough to warrant a word of its own, not just a My Chemical Romance song. I've always understood the song 'Teenagers' as a rallying cry for bad kids to band together against the ridiculous fears of the adult ruling class. Gerard Way wrote the song after being spooked by a group of rowdy teenagers on the subway. The encounter left him wondering if, given his stature in youth culture, he must be part of the problem; more deeply, his reaction signified his own departure from youth. He was now the scariest thing possible: old.

But as much as they may disturb us, we cannot look away from teens. Whole industries can't afford to – Gen Z accounts for roughly one-third of the world's population and spending power. While we cringe at how they navigate (or misuse) technology, the institutions and companies undergirding modern life are morphing to meet teens where they're at. Take news organizations' move to platforms like TikTok, for example, or how major fashion brands are, depressingly and successfully, selling virtual clothes to kids on the Roblox video game metaverse. From the Beatles to the KarJenners and everyone they've employed offstage, many rich people would not be rich without the buy-in of teenagers, particularly teenage girls.

None of this would matter if not for the existential magnetism of the teenager, the reason we're so obsessed with pontificating about them in the first place. They possess the youthful idiocy we've already lost forever. They're bound to replace us, hopefully take care of us. Their future – *our* future – lies in their ability to not fuck this all up. This must be why adults talk to and about teenagers differently from how they talk to slightly younger children, how we offer them more responsibility all while being more punitive of their behaviours. We can see the adults they are about to become, yet there is still time, theoretically, to fix them, a desire that's not pure altruism. Who would I be if someone older, someone who had a better understanding of the path ahead, had turned my shoulders in a slightly different direction? Like, even just forcing me to put money in a TFSA earlier – not that I would have listened.

I have recently started teaching high school, which has only heightened my personal hysteria over young people. I don't let them tell me what they did over the weekend, mostly because I can't handle imagining the spectacular ways teenagers flirt with danger. I love them, so I want to crawl into their brains and command them to spend their evenings sitting somewhere soft and indoors, or to put on a helmet before barrelling down the mountain. But I love them, so I would never want them to change. At some point, I decided that not giving kids advice unless they explicitly ask for it is the caring thing to do. This could be just as selfish as scolding them, born out of my own assumption that I would be a better-adjusted adult if I had felt just as much love after fucking up as I did after being good.

Getting older is so cruel. Once we have enough self-awareness to see where things went wrong, our present selves can only endure and repair, but never disappear, the spectre of our pasts. Projecting all of this onto young people isn't fair, but we do it anyway. How else can we help ourselves? Trying to change a teenager is the closest we come to turning the clocks back, to saving who we have become.

———

Teenagers, like malls, are an invention. Not coincidentally, the two emerged out of the same social and historical cauldron. I mean, people have been turning fifteen forever, but teenagers were never really considered a category and culture of their own as we currently know them until the years shortly before and following World War II. For the first time, the majority of North American kids were going to school instead of spending their days alongside adults in a factory, on the farm, or at war. They had free time to spend with people their own age, and they could drive. Plus, these kids' parents were having fewer of them and making more money; families could now spend beyond the bare necessities of keeping their brood housed and fed. Conspicuous consumption wasn't a new phenomenon in the 1950s – sociologists had been talking about the European leisure class for decades – but now, a sizable chunk of North Americans had enough money to buy rich-looking things for the sake of looking rich. The result was a new category of almost-adults who had time to kill and money to blow. Scientists were just beginning to generate data to validate earlier theories regarding the physical and psychological differences between children and adults. (Puberty standards for girls and boys, for example, weren't published until 1970.) In the 1930s, before anyone else, department stores used the word *teenager* in print, as clothing manufacturers began making items in between children's and women's sizes; it would be nearly a decade before the word translated into other contexts and began appearing in newspaper editorial copy. In many ways, then, teenagers were more clearly defined as consumers before they were understood as individuals.

Launched in 1944, *Seventeen* magazine was the first to capture a large teenage readership and conceptualize it as an emerging consumer group. According to its publishers' own accounts, the magazine was created in response to the growing teen market and a recognition of young people's wartime cultural consciousness. Publisher Walter Annenberg recalled walking past storefronts of teen girls' clothes on Fifth Avenue and remarking that a magazine did not yet exist for the age group. Helen Valentine, the magazine's founder and editor-in-chief, had a more sentimental attachment and motivation for creating it, having raised a teenage daughter herself and seen young people's engagement with the news. She thought that teen girls were neglected by the major publications of the day – not just as potential shoppers, but as serious consumers of politics and culture. A magazine designed just for teenage girls was a way of recognizing their full personhood. 'Everyone treats them as though they were silly, swooning bobby soxers,' Valentine said in a retrospective interview. 'I think they're young adults and should be treated accordingly.'

Valentine's more progressive vision for the magazine was more or less trumped by the publisher's doggedness in staking a claim in the media landscape. To familiarize advertisers with what felt like a slippery and unfamiliar target, the magazine created Teena: a fictional, prototypical teenage girl and *Seventeen* reader. Designed using data from surveys of American teen girls, Teena was the sixteen-year-old middle-class daughter of a businessman and stay-at-home mom. She liked shopping, going to the movies, and using makeup. She had a babysitting job, too, priming her with money to spend on whatever products in *Seventeen* spoke to her. In postcards sent to advertisers, the magazine reminded them that Teena wasn't alone – a million other *Seventeen* readers just like her were sprinkled across the country.

Seventeen characterized itself as Teena's cooler surrogate mother, her sounding board on everything from choosing the best lipstick for her skin tone to navigating her first crush. In turn, the magazine boasted Teena as the future of consumerism itself. Teena, after all, came of age in the commodity shortages of the war; she didn't have the brand loyalties of her mother, making her an early, impressionable investment toward a lifetime of brand loyalty. 'Teena the girl with a future can be your future too,' one postcard says, 'if you sell her in the magazine she and her teen-mates beg, borrow and buy – *Seventeen*.'

The emergence of teenagers, especially the girl ones, marked a monumental shift for the producers of commodities: a whole new category of people to sell clothes and makeup to. But the distinct material youth culture emerging out of the postwar period widened the chasm between adults and their children. Young people spent their time and formed their identities in increasingly mysterious ways – culturally, there had never been a greater threat to the age of majority's established social order.

People have been lamenting the bad behaviour of young people since the dawn of humanity; early English common law recognized that kids as young as seven had the capacity for *mens rea* that became comparable to an adult's by the time they turned fourteen. Juvenile delinquency, as the cultural concept that we recognize today, fully came to a head during the mid-century. The number of crimes committed by young people in the U.S. and Canada had increased steadily since the end of the war. The teenagers in the fifties seemed more violent as well; newspapers told horror stories of American teens making guns from car antennas, or joining the National Guard just to steal and use service pistols. This all poked at the already-sensitive Western identity as North America sulked into the Cold War. Teenagers were burdened with the responsibility of reflecting the values of a new world. The image of a nation teeming with lazy, delinquent youth didn't jive with the ideal of a strong and productive West. Academics at the time did, in fact, draw connections between social conditions, such as excessive free time, parents absented by work and war, poverty, racial segregation, and police surveillance itself, as driving factors behind youth crime.

Some have drawn connections between the mid-century segregation of housing, the 'white flight' to the suburbs, and government abandonment of urban centres newly disproportionately occupied by the poor and racialized. Most blatantly: the homes in mass-produced suburbs subsidized by the United States' 1949 housing program were only permitted to be bought by white people. Capital (and care) flowed away from the spaces where people were densely occupied. In a tale as old as time, news stories, and so our formal historical record, often skipped over documenting the organized resistance of tenants and workers in these communities for better conditions. The story we're more familiar with is the chaotically unappealing inner city, an inaccurate way to describe the manifestation of a system as designed: racist urban planning, under-resourcing, and overpolicing.

But more mainstream discourses – and even our current retelling of this history – latch on to the corruptible influence of a new mass-consumer-oriented media. If advertisements could influence teenagers to act a certain way, why wouldn't other, more morally bankrupt, media do the same? Comic books were among the first targets. In his 1954 bestseller, *Seduction of the Innocent*, psychiatrist Fredric Wertham drew upon his experience with troubled, racialized kids in New York City (and a questionable application of the scientific method) to illustrate the connection between violence in comic books and juvenile delinquency. Reading about Batman and Robin's suspicious homoeroticism could turn someone's son gay, for example, while Wonder Woman could transform an impressionable girl into an aggressive, man-hating lesbian.

Taking a closer look at the interviews in Wertham's book, however, reveals a more touching portrait of underprivileged kids reaching for agency in their lives. One thirteen-year-old girl, examined by Wertham due to her track record of 'truancy and disobedience,' says she likes the Sheena comics for the protagonist's fighting style: 'she fights like a man, swings on the vines, and kicks people in the face.' Wertham depicts children as young as twelve engaged in street prostitution and injecting heroin; his accounts of children living in extreme poverty and suffering mistreatment are genuinely disturbing. It's hard not to read their (sometimes brutal) acts of violence as an attempt to assert their own humanity, to impress upon otherwise impermeable forces of circumstance.

In 1953, the American senate established a subcommittee solely dedicated to investigating the driving factors of juvenile delinquency. Months later, Wertham spoke at the committee's two-day hearing on comic books, in which he claimed that the industry's methods for influencing young minds were more sophisticated than Hitler's. Public outcry stemming from the hearings compelled major comics publishers to establish the Code of the Comics Magazine Association of America, which restricted comics from depicting detailed violence, disrespect for authority, and even certain types of dress. Although he never endorsed it (and later denounced it outright), Wertham played a major role in establishing this cultural landmark in comics publishing. Later, he was able to recognize comic books' potential for good – his bigger beef was with the comics industry's exploitation of children's impressionability for profit, a more significant societal failure than a superhero inspiring one kid to pick up a knife.

Ever since, consumer choices have become shorthand for kids gone bad. Aesthetics make a clear target for moral panic. For youth, dressing a certain way gives you licence to enter a cool new social group. For adults, monitoring trends and their cultural signifiers is an act of (xenophobic, fake) self-protection. If you spot a kid walking toward you with a weird haircut, you can cross the street before getting mugged. If your daughter comes home wearing more eyeliner than usual, you can intervene before the wrong friend group sweeps her away.

The term *moral panic* itself wouldn't even exist without teen subcultures. Sociologist Stanley Cohen coined the term in 1972 to describe the British public's fear of the affluent, jazz-loving mods and leather-jacket-wearing rockers in the sixties and seventies. According to Cohen, a moral panic ensues when a social group threatens established social values. Aesthetics and mass media offer an easy shorthand to identify, and proliferate panic about, that group in unnuanced news reports, frightening all those parents who were living in relative peace before seeing a fateful article online or a segment on CNN. Suddenly, their child's collection of plastic bracelets from Claire's represents a dark energy slinking underneath a seemingly innocent sartorial choice. On one level, it means that their kid is a goth sex freak. Even worse, it reveals the chasm between what one can know about their child and what one can't.

And so youth aesthetics have become an urgent early indicator of youth deviance. Maybe your parents wrung their hands over your Marilyn Manson poster and *Call of Duty* obsession, the same panic your grandma projected on your dad's leather jacket and switchblade. Your daughter could have been acting slutty for many reasons. One of them could be that she saw Britney Spears wearing a miniskirt on MTV.

———

The shopping mall was destined to become the concerned parent's worst nightmare about their modern teenage child: a contained structure for youth to shop for those mysterious, potentially corrupting aesthetics and run wild beyond the gaze of a disciplinary adult.

This is ironic when you consider how many of our first trips to the mall were against our own will: being dragged, screaming and crying, to sit on the lap of a bearded stranger.

Real-life Santas – and the cultural memory of whispering our material desires in a stranger's ear – predate malls themselves. Department stores like Macy's were known to have hosted Santas as early as the 1850s and started hosting paid and photographed meet-and-greets by the 1940s.

The phrase *mall rat* popped up much later, in the late eighties. As the growth of malls exploded across North America, news articles employed the term while examining the new breed of mall-goers as an anthropological anomaly. The coverage articulated a fascination with how the kids presented themselves: their leather jackets, spiky hair, and disaffected 'tude – all markedly different, apparently, from how kids had looked before.

Mall rats were distinct from other shoppers because they weren't good at it. Loitering in the food court instead of packing up and heading to the next store, if not actually stealing from the store, is to resist the productivity the mall insists upon. The annoyance of this early writing about mall rats is tinged with sympathy for their empty youth. Consumerism seemed to be cheapening an essential feature of their lives – they were now hyper-focused on how they looked, arranging themselves into seemingly meaningless social groups dictated by their dress. The phenomenon had everything to do with the mall's enclosed physicality. In 1981, an Associated Press article mused that, thanks to the shopping centre and the computer chip, 'suburban American teen-agers may never again know the heat of summer.' People were eating out more and playing video games. The material reality of being a young person was abstracted far beyond what had been experienced by the generation before.

After the cultural throat-clearing, mall rats usually made the news only for breaking the law: stealing, beating up other kids, booting liquor, and selling coke to thirteen-year-olds. In 1986, after Canadian prostitution solicitation laws got tougher, the *Globe and Mail* reported that young male sex workers were turning to Toronto malls to turn tricks more subtly. The crowds and public bathrooms offered less exposure than the open streets. Malls became a magnet for under-the-radar crime, and there seemed to be few options to control it beyond increasing security and handing out trespassing charges.

West Edmonton Mall's stature didn't quell local adults' mall-rat anxieties. The world's largest, most labyrinthine mall, one could assume, would be crawling with runaways, drug dealers, and pimps hungry for straightlaced kids to seduce into a dark underworld. The structure of the gigantic mall only added to its urban-legend allure. Most of its doors were open twenty-four hours a day, so homeless kids had seamless access to sleep, among other things, in the vast corridors used by mall employees. The mall was a fitting sign of the times, with the mall rats as a bonus extended metaphor: literally scurrying out of view, tunnelling under and eroding the mall's structural integrity, the mall's (the society's!) moral integrity. Reading stories from this time makes me nostalgic for the giddy flourish of newspaper reporting. One reporter called the mall a 'kaleidoscope of sensations and possibilities that caters to the most outrageous whim, home to fantasy-makers peddling hashish and promises to young girls.' Prose!

The actual violence going on at the mall didn't help with its image. Teens were robbing people with pepper spray, ripping pay phones off walls, beating people with baseball bats. Once, a teenager blew up a locker at Galaxyland. Later, a seventeen-year-old was sentenced to eight years after hitting and dragging a police officer with a stolen truck in the mall parking lot. Another police officer found an eighteen-year-old living in a crawlspace between two levels, with $62,000 of merchandise he had stolen by dropping into stores' ceiling vents. By the nineties, the mall was having about ten break-ins each month and hosted the highest number of juvenile delinquent charges in the city. In 1992, a nineteen-year-old was chased out of the mall and attacked by a group of twenty bat-wielding teenagers.

This trend was consistent among other malls. Several studies in the eighties and nineties found that crime rates in a neighbourhood increased when a mall was built in it, due in no small part to the influx of unsupervised youth it brought into the area. In its first year, the Mall of America accounted for 10 per cent of calls to the police department in Bloomington, Minnesota. The majority of people arrested in the early days at the mall were teenagers; not surprisingly, a significant number of calls were motivated by racism alone, reporting a Black person walking around the mall in a way a white person found suspicious. Some of the crimes were more scandalous than others: six months after the Mall of America opened, three people were shot in its Camp Snoopy amusement park when a group of young people attempted to steal a jersey from a thirteen-year-old boy.

Incidents like these raised the question of what malls could possibly do to curb teen misbehaviour. The Mall of America unsuccessfully experimented with making the lights brighter at the amusement park. West Edmonton Mall started locking its entrance doors at night in 1992. The move seemed inspired less by the violence itself than by the fact that the *Edmonton Journal* ran a series of stories illustrating the shocking livelihoods of the two hundred or so mall rats spending their days there. The food-court cliques – called the Rappers, Funkers, Socials, and Preppies – led the reporter on a two-month journey through the mall's underworld, narrating drug deals and sex lives in the back corridors. Among them were bored middle-class kids and homeless dropouts, an eighteen-year-old nicknamed Grandma who had been hanging out at the mall since she was ten, and a Galaxyland employee who lived and dealt drugs in the mall for five months.

The mall rats pointed to a bigger issue in the city. A 1992 city report found that more than 80 per cent of property crimes were committed by young adults aged fifteen to twenty-four, mostly unemployed, poor high school dropouts. People were also particularly worried about teenage girls, as they represented the fastest-growing population of smokers in North America. Once the mall began locking more entrance doors at night and beefing up security, a new complaint followed. West Edmonton residents were pissed because the teens driven out of the mall were now vandalizing their neighbourhoods. The mall's chapel and a storefront school tried to reach them, but it seemed like nothing could get to the root of the mall-rat problem. Mall cops pointed at Triple Five, calling for better security measures. Triple Five pointed at parents, arguing that families were using the space as a free babysitter and that the same issue happened at other malls – West Edmonton

Mall, they argued, got more attention only because it was the biggest. If you zoom back, the spat looks like a collective throwing of hands in the air. The overwhelming sentiment was that the teens were squandering something: their time, their youth. Not much imagination was applied toward where kids could possibly go, other than their homes or schools, or why those wouldn't be viable places to grow up.

The *Journal* articles, however, do emphasize the appeal of the mall. Most obviously, the size and secrecy lent access to drugs and cigarettes, even leftover food from people's trays in the food court. But one girl, a mainstay at the Phase I Gourmet World food court, told a reporter that the mall rats came here as a place to make friends and because, as she said, 'it's warm inside … Everybody here is brother and sister to each other. It's like a family.'

Although my own use of the mall looked different, I doubt my core motivation was any different from that of the kids in these articles; we went there (and to everyone's annoyance, stayed there) for the same reasons. The shared experience of being a teenager is being halfway under the thumb of something or someone larger than you. The actions we take at that age represent a calculation between our increasing awareness of that weight and the means available to do something about it. The mall was, and still is, a space of agency during the frustration of that liminal time. Whether they were getting a shirt at Hot Topic or making a home out of the tunnels beneath it, the mall may have been the only place that offered self-invention on a young person's own terms.

———

My local mall, St. Albert Centre, has always been pretty shitty. It did not have great mall-rat potential: a single-level tube of mediocre retail, more of a last resort than a destination in itself. Intentionally visiting this mall was usually a last-minute act of desperation before a school dance. We would bypass Northern Reflections (where moms bought those frumpy sweatshirts with loons on them) and the Bay to try to find something at Winners or Bootlegger. Nothing, however, compared with the seemingly limitless cosmopolitan selection at West Edmonton Mall's Forever 21.

To be honest, I didn't have great mall-rat potential, either. My first instinct is to tell you that I was too obsessed with being good to be a mall rat. I can't overstate what a great life my parents gave me, but that didn't predispose me toward becoming particularly cool. I attended a Baptist church, for example. I committed D.A.R.E. programming gravely and unironically to heart and had to take Ukrainian folk-dancing lessons instead of jazz. Really, I think being privileged and a loner had more to do with my lack of mall-rat status. My house was safe and stable; I spent my waking hours preoccupied with riding horses, feeding my Neopets, and quietly avoiding the eternal damnation that awaited my godless best friends. You know, the classic chicken/egg of being uncool and sexually repressed! Nature, nurture, whatever – it all hardwired me for that incel-lite, not-like-other-girls vibe of the early 2000s. I revelled in not being a slacker or a slut, poorly hiding how much I wanted to be three things: relaxed, beautiful, invited to smoke behind the school.

Longing was my most definitive feeling, which must be why West Edmonton Mall was such a palace to me as a teenager. For one, it was a twenty-minute drive from my house, long enough that going there felt like a small occasion, short enough that I knew I could always go back. The sheer number of stores and things to do allowed the mall to mirror the huge fantasies I had about myself. I didn't have a specific idea of who I wanted to become. I didn't care, as long as I was moving toward an improvement of my current self. This felt like a dauntingly ambiguous task before Instagram became a thing. The mall was the third and final source, in addition to people at school and magazines, of ideas of what I could look like. When you spend a lot of time in your own mind, the mall is an altar for becoming – for me, the mall promised to deliver every possible permutation of that future-person, whether she was an Abercrombie-wearing puck bunny or a girl standing in the indoor wave pool with her boyfriend.

I was fifteen and believed my personal lack of money was what prevented me from being more comfortable in my skin. Of course, this meant that the dream of inventing myself at the mall never came true – I always left with my particular wish being only partially fulfilled. (As the old adage goes, you can get a full-priced Aritzia hoodie with your first paycheque and still self-mythologize your social awkwardness.) I am no longer fifteen, but I still have to remind myself that you can never actually finish the job of inventing yourself through buying the right things. If that was the case, the mall would have closed long before I was even born; I wouldn't have, seconds ago, bookmarked a TikTok sharing the affirmation that *nothing I buy will spiritually fulfill me*.

One of the best days of my life in junior high, though, was in the last month of Grade 9, when my school rewarded everyone who had decent grades and good attendance with a trip to the World Waterpark. Looking back, aspects of the day were kind of pathetic, namely the part where I watched my best friend make out with my crush in the wave pool. I could have thrown up (I had never seen tongues do that before) but 'Don't Stop Believin'' was reverberating over the fishbowl-like dome encasing us, and everyone around me was singing along, flooding the moment with a sense of importance: here we are, perfectly reciting the same words our parents know, announcing our place in the great big culture. In the photos taken on my friend's waterproof disposable camera at the top of the slides, I was clearly uncomfortable in myself, angling my face and body in the one way I thought looked acceptably documentable. My smile, though, was genuine. A few weeks later, I would go to my first actual house party; for now, this moment was the only time I had been out in the world, unsupervised, with more than a couple of close friends – with girls *and* guys. After being essentially friendless at the beginning of the school year, I started to see myself in the contours of a group of people getting older. I had no makeup on, and my hair was wet and matted. I didn't yet know what it meant to be myself, let alone that being myself was something to enjoy, but on this day, I began to understand who I could become.

———

If you opened an Edmonton newspaper in 2005 you would likely see a photo of Nina Courtepatte, a thirteen-year-old

Cree girl with a bright smile, her hair pulled back into a bouncy ponytail. In the articles following her death, Courtepatte's mother said the girl loved *Canadian Idol* and *America's Next Top Model* and had her sights set on becoming a model herself. In 2004, she won a local modelling contest.

Courtepatte and her best friend had been hanging out at the arcade in West Edmonton Mall when a group of self-described mall rats – two adult men, three teenagers – invited them to a bush party. What follows is an awful story: Courtepatte was beaten with a wrench and sexually assaulted twice before being bludgeoned to death with a sledgehammer. Eventually, the five people were convicted in her sexual assault and murder, but not before Courtepatte's family were forced to endure a series of court cases that sprawled into the years after her death. The ordeal was arduous and hard to follow, due largely to the killers' lies and cover-ups, later admissions, and own narratives of traumatic upbringings, the abuse that led many of them to find shelter and a sense of belonging in the mall. The sensational stories tugged attention away from the singular tragedy of Courtepatte's life being taken so violently and unfairly. One of the teen girls responsible for killing Courtepatte, for example, was interested in the occult, burning Bibles, and drinking blood – she cleaned the murder weapons in the Zellers bathroom before selling them to pay for a tarot card reading.

Two months before Courtepatte's death, Rene Gunning, who was nineteen, and Krystle Knott, who was sixteen, were last seen at West Edmonton Mall before they disappeared. The girls, who were both Indigenous and from Northern B.C., had met that day through mutual friends near the Ice

Palace. After they'd all been drinking in the parking lot, the other members of their group left for a house party, while Gunning and Knott hung around. The two called their friends from a pay phone later that night – the mall was closing, they were getting kicked out, and they couldn't get a ride to the party, so they decided to hitchhike back to Fort St. John. It was the last time anyone heard from them.

Although Gunning's disappearance made the news in 2005, Knott's wasn't announced or publicly linked to hers until 2008. Their remains were found in 2011 near Grande Prairie, about a four-hour drive from Edmonton. Their killer has never been caught. Announcements about Gunning's and Knott's disappearances overlapped with coverage of Courtepatte's killers' trials, reinvigorating another discourse about the state of today's youth and the role of the mall in it all. Once again, articles illustrated the impossibility of reining in the mall rats: the drugs and weapons police found on baby-faced loiterers, the kids who stole by swarming unassuming shoppers. One *Edmonton Journal* article even noted that 'all' of the swarmers were 'from ethnic backgrounds.' The article cites Gunning, Knott, and Courtepatte's cases as evidence of the mall's violence. It doesn't end, however, before noting that Gunning and Knott were on an RCMP list of missing people who led 'high-risk' lifestyles, and noting recent crimes other girls had committed at the mall.

'But girls are not always victims,' the article states, one line after detailing Gunning's, Knott's, and Courtepatte's cases. 'Police receive reports of girls robbed by other girls in mall washrooms, or girls making a grab for the purses of unsuspecting women in store change rooms. This past spring, three 13-year-old girls allegedly pressed knives to the bellies of their victims.'

The article stops short of blaming Gunning, Knott, and Courtepatte for the cruelty strangers inflicted upon them. At the same time, it hardly lets the tragedy, or the reader's perception of Gunning's, Knott's, and Courtepatte's innocence, hang in the air before skewering the halo above their heads. To be mall rats, the article's logic suggests, was to choose the risk of, if not culpability for, violence.

Years later, you could finally find stories about who these missing girls were and about the families kept up at night longing for their return. Until then, they were broadly and inhumanely portrayed as metaphors for the worst outcomes of a dangerous mall and careless youth – no mention, obviously, of the colonial logic that treasures an Indigenous girl's life less than a white one's.

Instead, we heard about the ills of absent parents, gangs, video games, and the police's inability to keep up with it all. In 2008, the police department kept a flow chart of the teenagers arrested in the mall, connecting friends, siblings, and gangs and tracking when kids were scheduled to leave the young offenders' centre. They'd share this information with security guards at West Edmonton Mall, but they still couldn't keep the problem under control. In an *Edmonton Journal* article detailing this strategy, a police officer likens the kids to vermin: you could never get rid of them, only displace the issue to somewhere else. They also had an ingrained hatred of cops and authority, apparently baked into their genes by their authority-hating parents, which they were destined to recreate as they grew older and had families of their own.

'It perpetuates,' one cop said in the same article. 'And then they're gonna go and procreate. Bah. I'll be retired.'

But on Friday nights, as people were asking God what could be done about the West Edmonton Mall rats, four hundred teenagers bumped and grinded to R. Kelly at Rush, the mall's underage nightclub, and partied at Rock 'n' Ride, a monthly teen rave held in Galaxyland.

Even beyond the huge attractions – the amusement park, waterpark, and stores – nearly every corner of the mall has always actively attracted teenagers to visit it. In 1999, eight thousand teens crammed into the mall to vie for Britney Spears's signature, and they came back a year later to watch the Spice Girls' Mel C perform at the HMV Stage. For a while, the mall even had a children's board of directors, which allowed kids to offer feedback about elements that they liked and disliked. (We had them to thank for naming Fisher, Sea Life Caverns' penguin mascot, and for a conveyor belt that hauled sleds to the top of one of the slides in the waterpark.)

For every detectable moral panic, you could find a way that the mall welcomed it, facilitated it, and made money from it. In the early 2000s, local police were starting to freak out about sex bracelets and the internet, blaming 'computer chat rooms' for as much as 80 per cent of incidents that involved young people and required police intervention. And yet, the mall still fully embraced the internet to capitalize on the draw of burgeoning online communities, acting as a portal between virtual and real worlds. Circuit Circus, an arcade and internet café close to Galaxyland, was once open twenty-four hours a day. Around the corner, Blueshift Gaming was one of the only places you could buy Nexopia Plus, the upgraded version of the social media platform all young Edmontonians used before making the great migration to Facebook.

—————

I never went to Rock 'n' Ride. It sounded fun: for fifteen dollars each, two thousand teens got unlimited rides until midnight while enjoying the impeccable vibes of a Much Video Dance. But by my friend's snobby St. Albert standards, Rock 'n' Ride was synonymous with street drugs and scene kids – the emo-adjacent Myspace-core subculture known for their deep side parts and eyeliner. Until the last couple of years of high school, most of us were pretty pearl-clutchy. For example, nobody thought it was cool when word got around that someone in our grade was dabbling in ketamine; people thought the guy was a scene freak and spread a school-wide rumour that he was sexually into horses.

Meanwhile, I was secretly in awe of scene kids. I'd spend hours poring over their Nexopia Plus profiles, these meticulously designed spreads of bright hex codes, photo shoots, and song lyrics from bands I had never heard of. To me, scene kids had unlocked an underground aesthetic language – I couldn't comprehend where they got the money or knowledge to style themselves that way. It would still be several years before beauty tutorials infiltrated YouTube or I scoured Tumblr to learn more than one way of dressing. Until then, I solely relied on the narrow avenue of my friends and *Seventeen* magazine to teach me where to shop and how to do my hair. For years, I tried in vain to ask my grandmotherly hairdresser for cool side bangs; I once cut a pair of underwear into a thong because I couldn't muster the courage to ask my mom to buy me one. Scene kids seemed to be the only ones who were expressing themselves through their appearances. Cool, in retrospect, but weird to normie eighth-graders.

The mall shut down Rock 'n' Ride in 2009 after Cassie Williams, a fourteen-year-old Grade 9 student, died of an accidental drug overdose. While waiting to get into Rock 'n' Ride, Williams and her friend bought six ecstasy pills each, folded them into a napkin, and stuffed them under her bra. The girls collapsed under the roller coasters before nine o'clock that night. Her friend would recover, but Williams was taken off life support the next day, her mother standing beside her. The seventeen-year-old dealer was given a four-month jail sentence, a landmark decision because it was the first time a minor in the province had been incarcerated for dealing ecstasy.

Williams's friends said she had a beautiful voice and that she was supposed to attend the performing arts high school the next year. With dip-dyed pink hair and bold makeup, she was the epitome of the Nexopia cool girl I would have idolized. Her memorial Facebook page is a time capsule to the stylized web-speak of the time:

> rest in peace beautiful ♥
> Miss youu., I kknow you can see uss., .
> Id take your placee if i coulld., ILYSM

Williams died before she was able to fully come into herself – the most unfair thing about losing someone so young to what must be preventable. Infinite alternate realities spin out from editing just one scene from her night. What if she had taken one pill instead of six? What if the dealer had got caught before he got to her? What if there had been no party, no mall?

A similar set of questions could be asked about each of the girls whose deaths have been connected to the mall. Was it just a backdrop to the events that took these girls' lives? Or did it play an active role in initiating their deaths?

We know, after all, that the mall presented a unique space for teenagers to come together like never before. There must be a way to also understand the same space as a focalizer for harm; there must also be a way to do this without stripping these people of their humanity and agency, as many of the moral-panic discourses around them did. To zoom out beyond both the structure of the mall and the structure of the teenager, it becomes clear that they were created by the same conditions of history. Both malls and the whole industry of teenage consumption emerged to respond to a class of people with more disposable income than ever before. The same era's neoliberal policy and white flight drove families and communities into isolation from one another. To criticize teenagers for being materialistic or vapid or reckless misses the true tragedy of this generational category. If the teenage girl was invented as a vessel for consumption, the value of her existence is measured by what she makes of herself, what she can afford.

Or maybe malls aren't appropriate to mention alongside these tragedies at all – malls, after all, didn't invent poverty or the violence it inspires. If we make their deaths about a mall, do we reduce the beginning and ending of their lives, each precious and irretrievable, to mere structural inevitabilities?

None of this changes the fact that there is no timeline where malls exist without the teenager. And, to be very precise, there is no timeline where the mall, or teenage culture, exists without the teenage girl. When a teenage girl dies in a mall, she dies in a place explicitly designed for her becoming. This is either the greatest betrayal or a machine merely revealing its design.

———

Grief has a different texture now that we have public venues to work through this incomprehensibility. Every untimely death becomes a discursive opportunity; the concept of responsibility takes the shape of a shield. In addition to sweet messages, Williams's memorial page on Facebook became a platform for debate and subtle scolding, kids blaming other kids for faking grief for attention, adults warning teenagers to not be 'E-tards' and calling on the mall to do something, fucking anything, to prevent this from happening again. After all, everyone knew kids were coming to Rock 'n' Ride to get high; it was only a matter of time before something like this happened. Dozens of stories, editorials, and letters to the editor in Edmonton papers reckoned with the same ideas: if only the mall had drug dogs, if only more parents talked to their kids about drugs, if only teenagers realized they weren't invincible. 'Maybe if more parents were actively parenting and not allowing their kids to do things they should not,' one letter goes, 'the scum that these events attract would just go away.'

I can't write about these stories without remembering how, when I was a teenager, my own thoughts mirrored this reflexive armour – that my lonely, small-feeling life was somehow justified by what I understood to be its safety. Growing up, I devoured the *Edmonton Sun* every morning as I ate my breakfast, reading updates on the trial of Courtepatte's killers alongside the newspaper's conservative punditry and hysterically moralizing retellings of other crimes. This was the only newspaper I read.

I was just two years younger than Courtepatte and one year older than Williams when I read about their deaths. I wish I could say the coverage made me anxious, made me swear off the mall, made me newly afraid of strangers or public spaces. But none of it scared me away from going to the mall. I didn't feel like the warnings applied to me. On one hand, all spaces, including malls, are disproportionately less dangerous for a white kid living in a safe home. I didn't know that at the time, though. What I did believe was that the difference between me and them came down to my own ability to make good choices – as if I had the capacity or opportunity to choose anything consequential; as if any of the things I read about were the result of anything that resembled choice. What haunts me now is how close I could be to a tragedy and feel nothing. I believed I had nothing in common with two girls my age looking for some version of the same thing.

———

The speaker in American poet Tony Hoagland's poem 'At the Galleria Shopping Mall' watches his nine-year-old niece declare that her favourite sport is shopping. And just like that, she loses the innocent, pre-materialist version of herself.

'So let it begin,' Hoagland writes:

As the gods in olden stories

turned mortals into laurel trees and crows
    to teach them some kind of lesson,

so we were turned into Americans
to learn something about loneliness.

Hoagland's poem captures a greater anxiety regarding young people's involvement in consumerism, albeit with a different flavour from the moral panics I described earlier. This girl's fondness for shopping doesn't have anything to do with an authority-eroding subculture but rather her departure from a more pure engagement with the world. She departs from truth and forever enters the lonely American machine.

I felt prickly when I first read the poem. Over the past decade, critics and academics have done a good job documenting how our culture trivializes the interests of women and girls, not to mention young people in general. Conceptions of capitalism, throughout its evolution since the eighteenth century, have valued producer-side roles as useful and masculine, the apparent foundation of society and the home. And, although there would be no market without consumption, it's long been constructed as the insatiable feminine domain – a task to be reined in by the rational man of the house.

It follows, then, that things like clothes and makeup – and shopping for both – are easily cast aside as frivolous, even corrupting to a girl's true potential. (If you follow this thought further, this 'true potential' is probably something about her being a good producer: a good mother or good employee.) This thinking disregards the creativity, intelligence, and complex inventions of self that are involved in the motions of being a girl. Makeup isn't just a tool for submitting to the male gaze, for example, but can be wielded to subvert it. Cutting my underwear into the world's worst thong could have been a determinative act of early sexual agency, carving out my own destiny as a woman who no longer has panty lines. Or we might consider the liberating elements of a shopping mall – a place where a girl can aesthetically depart from the ideals her parents have for her, or move freely outside of the home. If she's loitering or shoplifting, she's actively resisting norms of how people are expected to behave in a public space. Or something like that.

After writing it all out, I wonder: Are we cool with this? I appreciate how thoroughly people validate the textures of life under capitalism, to make it feel like it's not a colossal waste of oxygen and carbon and, like, human spirit. But, again: Are we cool with this? I feel sad when I'm at a restaurant and see a baby on an iPad! When the teenager in front of me at a concert spends the whole time on his phone, a small part of me dies. That's not just a figure of speech – I feel like something integral to my own soul has been lost for them. Then I wonder which adults I've made sad through my own engagements with modern life, what things were lost before I could appreciate them. Right now, I can't unsee the disappointment in my grandfather's eyes meeting mine as I put down my phone, unsure of how long he was waiting to talk to me.

Capitalism requires an acceleration and novelty that makes Hoagland's initial qualm with malls already feel quaint. Shopping and babies on iPads, I'd argue in the least parent-shaming way possible, all exist along the same continuum, a history that now predates each of us: as the market increasingly infiltrates our lives, our real lives become less interesting versions of what's happening in our personal metaverses. I'm not even sure why I bother thinking about this sometimes – if being cool or uncool about it matters at all. Like, is there anything I can do about it, as a non-billionaire, let alone as someone with no assets?

For the sake of all of us, I'll stop there. It's basically suicidal to not see how a good, meaningful life can be lived here. It's immoral, politically useless, to not protect this life and work to make it better for people who don't have the space to luxuriate in all the ways the world sucks. If my grandfather were still alive, I would currently be texting him to apologize for texting in front of him all the time. You might have noticed this: when I'm spiralling or struggling to make a point, I revert to telling a story about myself, a compulsion I picked up as a teenager, oversharing to create the illusion of intimacy. I once thought I was doing it to put other people at ease, fast-forwarding the awkward process of getting to know one another by revealing too much too soon. Now I know it's always been about me. My desire to be understood, my obsession with trying to understand the point of all this if it's not going to heaven or having all your teachers thinking you're a pleasure to have in class. By speaking myself into the world, I will belong in the world. That's the hope. In reality, here I am: still writing, trying to seal up something meaningful in my brain.

With that being said, I can't end the chapter with you think-ing that I was weird and lonely forever. I drank and did drugs in high school! I left with more friends than I came with!

I had dramatic thoughts about the mall, but I had fun at the mall, too. Have you ever gone into a store with your friends, for example? Not to buy anything, but just to be funny and random? One time, when I was thirteen, we went to Party City at West Edmonton Mall to take photos of ourselves with my friend's digital camera. We spent what must have been an hour trying on weird costume hats and gigantic sunglasses, making ironic poses, passing the camera off to one another, lying on the floor. I'm sure we were laugh-ing. I think an employee eventually asked us to leave. The photos aren't on Facebook anymore, so I can't do a great job of describing what I looked like that afternoon. But, as if it happened today, I still clearly remember how I felt: I was so happy to be there with them. I wouldn't have changed a thing.

Animals

The most famous mall animal – or at least the only one with his own biographic feature film, children's books, and Wikipedia page – was Ivan, a gorilla who lived the majority of his life in the Tacoma, Washington, B&I shopping centre. The mall's owner bought Ivan from an exotic animal broker in 1964 after he was illegally captured as a baby in the Congo. Living with the family who ran the mall's pet store, he spent his early years wearing diapers, climbing walls, and being carried on their teenage sons' shoulders like an uncanny and hairy, but otherwise loved, human child. Inevitably, he grew too big, too animal, to live in a human bungalow. When the family left him at home alone, nothing they owned was safe from Ivan's ability to destroy; he stripped their furniture clean of its fabric, upended a tank of fish. Three years after arriving in Washington, Ivan was moved into a concrete enclosure at the B&I. He would be near, but never interact with, the mall's other resident exotic animals: a rotating cast including chimpanzees, a baby elephant, a lion, and a jaguar, none of whom lasted as long as Ivan.

He became a local celebrity, an asset in luring potential shoppers to the B&I; his move to the mall came shortly after a new interstate highway threatened the mall's foot traffic. Ivan didn't register on the national radar, though, until he was featured in a three-minute segment of *The Urban Gorilla*, a 1990 National Geographic documentary narrated by Glenn Close. The other animals in the film, all living in outdoor sanctuaries and zoos, cast Ivan in especially depressing relief. As shoppers peer through the glass into his enclosure, Ivan stares through one of the concrete walls, as if trying to find his reflection or a trap door. He ambles toward the glass, smacking it listlessly before skulking out of view.

The segment also features an interview with a vaguely apologetic Ron Irwin, who took over the mall's ownership after his father's passing. Irwin admitted that Ivan's life in the enclosure was far from ideal but said his hands were tied. He tried for twelve years, without luck, to find a female companion for Ivan. Girl gorillas were considered precious to zoo breeding programs. Nobody was willing to give them up, let alone banish them to a roadside mall. Plus, gorillas had become listed as an endangered species after Ivan had moved into the B&I; it was now illegal to capture any new gorillas to display for profit. Irwin didn't mention, however, that he turned down several offers from American zoos (and from Michael Jackson) to adopt Ivan and move him somewhere better. Irwin later claimed that Ivan didn't stand a chance of surviving the journey to a new place.

Ivan's story doesn't end in the worst way: he did get to leave the mall after the B&I filed for bankruptcy in 1992. He was evaluated as an asset worth $30,000 and was sold to a zoo. After twenty-five years inside, being recognized as an item of private property was his ticket to becoming an animal again. He then made his move to Zoo Atlanta. Hundreds of people were there to watch him take his first steps onto the lush grass of the Ford African Rain Forest, an enclosure named for the motor company that sponsored it.

———

In 2012, the same year Ivan died, the American writer Katherine Applegate published *The One and Only Ivan*, a children's novel loosely based on Ivan's life. The novel won the prestigious Newbery Medal and, in 2021, was adapted into a broadly panned movie written by Mike White and starring Bryan Cranston and Angelina Jolie.

No other mall animal has captured the same creative imagination. There's nothing too stirring, after all, about the inertia of animal life in a mall: a stressed baby goat in a temporary petting zoo, an inbred Shih Tzu in a pet store, a goldfish swimming in circles, perpetually assailed by pennies. Really, mall animals only get a narrative arc if they can escape. For a moment in 2022, it looked like a gorilla living alone in a Thailand mall was about to get an Ivan-style story. Bua Noi, a gorilla in her thirties, had lived the majority of her life on the seventh floor of the Pata Department Store in Bangkok, the last ten years in isolation after her mate died. After activists online collected more than 100,000 petition signatures to free Bua Noi, the Thai government offered to buy the gorilla and relocate her to the German zoo she was originally bought from. But the mall owners balked – like Ivan's original owners, they said that she would be unlikely to survive the journey over.

And even when mall animals get to escape, the end is never quite as neatly tied up as Ivan's. Take Pizza, dubbed 'the world's saddest polar bear' by what felt like a thousand content-farm articles, the most recent mall animal to be famously released. In 2017, Pizza was rescued from his solitary enclosure in Grandview Mall in Guangzhou, China, and returned to his birthplace, a zoo elsewhere in the country. The story fizzles out from there. It's not clear where Pizza is now or if this new home is any better than the mall. In either case, the Grandview Mall still has beluga whales and Arctic wolves, among other animals, living in its basement aquarium. Shoppers have recently photographed the two resident walruses out on walks around the mall, surrounded by a crowd enthusiastically pointing smart phones at them.

———

At West Edmonton Mall, it's not unusual to see a small, singular African penguin ambling around the feet of shoppers. I'm not sure why they let out only one at a time, but it gives the effect of a man who doesn't yet know that he was transformed into a bird, not quite sure when everyone became so tall, purposefully waddling toward the Bay nonetheless.

Fifteen or so African penguins live in Sea Life Caverns, the mall's underground aquarium, among touch pools where visitors can poke at anemones and bamboo sharks and watch sea turtles glide through tanks of salt water. The penguins, their species projected to become extinct by 2040, are the only ones that get momentary vacations from their tanks. In addition to their occasional trips around the mall, you can also hire them for events, like proposals or weddings.

The aquarium was built in the third phase of the mall's construction, in 1985. But even before that, animals have always played a role in manufacturing West Edmonton Mall's allure. Long-time Edmontonians talk about the mall's resident animals coming and going like mirages. Everyone remembers the dolphins, who performed in a tank beside the aquarium from 1985 to 2004, but there were also tigers, baby cougars and black bears, emus and ostriches, peacocks, a gold tank of piranhas. Hockey-playing chimpanzees entertained guests at the grand opening of Phase III. A monkey exhibit closed because they overbred themselves to the point of outgrowing their enclosure; a birdcage near a food court closed because so many people were throwing junk food in through the cage's open ceiling. One of the more depressing corners of the mall was recently home to Sloth World, where visitors could pay to hold sloths and boa constrictors. Before closing in 2023, it was among the handful of mall exhibits operated by Little Ray's Nature Centre.

————

It's a historical guarantee: where people go, animals follow. Still, of all the things about malls that perplex me, I can't wrap my head around the animals.

The inverse, zoo-as-money-spending-experience, makes sense to me. People like looking at animals; naturally, you could get super-rich letting people look at animals while selling them eighteen-dollar killer whale magnets. Watching another living being pace around an enclosure when you know their ancestors or even close cousins got to live freely doesn't feel great, but modern zoos do a good job nudging any of these bad vibes out of their visitors' peripheries. They have little signs with the words *research* and *conservation* emblazoned on them. Enclosures are usually full of plants and feature a couple of places to hide, not entirely unlike real life. And way safer, too. Zoos are free from poachers and deforestation, making them the least-bad unnatural place on the planet for animals to live. There's the promise that through preserving the animals here, they or their descendants will someday be released into the wild – and even if that never happens, the opportunity to gaze at animals potentially educates a new generation of nature lovers, ready to take up the baton to protect the environment of the future. Zoos are a comfort, an ark for our environmental anxieties, if not the actual survival of endangered species.

Quantifying the positive impact of zoos, however, is slippery. Good things do go down at zoos. The Toronto Zoo, for example, has bred and released more than five hundred Blanding's turtles into more than a hundred hectares of wild habitat they helped restore. The Vancouver Aquarium, which controversially displayed wild-caught belugas, is also home to the Marine Mammal Research Unit, which studies the well-being of orcas on the west coast.

In many other cases, however, the actual benefit to wild animals from research on captive animals is negligible. In 2016, a review commissioned by the Vancouver Humane Society and Zoocheck found that over the past thirty years, only thirteen peer-reviewed papers were published based on research on captive cetaceans at the Vancouver Aquarium, and most were not widely cited. Other reviews of zoo-based research have found that most academic articles published by zoos and aquariums are about animal husbandry: research to improve the living conditions of animals that currently live in zoos. Many of these studies cite animal well-being as an important way for zoos to maintain their credibility, and thus viability, as businesses. But then there's the catch: research costs money. How could zoo and aquarium research programs exist without admission fees?

Digging into zoos' roles in creating sustainable citizens comes up with similar results. Although most studies have found that zoo-goers will self-report to have more positive ideas about animals and the environment, virtually none of them have taken on a new conservation-related activity to protect the environment in their own lives. This reveals what we have all probably known to be true: the accoutrement of conservation doesn't fit well within the zoo's true calling as entertainer. One study of nearly two thousand American zoo visitors found that while the majority of zoo visitors made positive comments about animals in the enclosure, only slightly more than one-quarter read the exhibit's educational materials.

This is all without mentioning the things that make zoos more overtly fucked up. Modern zoos, especially in Europe, actively cull excess animals. Zoos in Denmark have made the news for this, having killed a lion and a baby giraffe to prevent inbreeding in their enclosures. Both animals were dissected before live audiences, and the giraffe's remains were thrown to the zoo's resident lions. None of this, in my opinion, is as heinous as the Cincinnati Zoo catapulting its (very cute) hippo Fiona to social-media stardom as a public-relations cleanup after killing Harambe the gorilla. Wake up, sheeple!

Peeling back the origins of animal captivity reveals a more sinister logic. British menageries, the earliest zoos, would display human beings and wild animals captured from colonies alongside one another – literal and metaphorical colonial domination of 'the exotic.' Then the menageries grew larger and became attached to scientific societies. In the early twentieth century, a German animal dealer was the first to create natural environments for his animals on display. He drew inspiration from the popularity of his 'people shows' toured across Europe and North America, in which he would dress and display captured Indigenous people in their cultural garb.

By the 1980s, as the conservation movement picked up speed, zoos responded by making their enclosures more natural and talking overtly about conservation. It all boded well for zoo attendance. The Denver Zoo doubled its revenue and the North Carolina Zoo nearly doubled its attendance after each spent $30 million on exhibits that allowed their animals to move around more naturally. In 1997, the American Association of Zoos and Aquariums reported that the widespread shift to these kinds of enclosures enticed more people to visit zoos and aquariums than attended all professional football, basketball, and baseball games combined that year.

In other words, zoos did not emerge as a response to natural habitats becoming less hospitable to wild animals. The zoos that we know today, with natural-looking environments and research programs, are rebrandings of darkly colonial power displays.

Animals-in-malls weren't even a separate invention from malls themselves. The very first mall, Gruen's Southdale Center in Minnesota, featured a petting zoo, in addition to a cage of exotic birds and a fish pond – attractions like any other, alongside the ice rink and carousel. In his own writing in 1952, Gruen stated that, in order for malls to function as 'a new outlet for that primary human instinct to mingle with other humans,' shopping centres should include not only stores, but greenhouses, art shows, and, yes, 'miniature zoos.' Although animals' inclusion might be categorically odd, the decision to have them or not seems to follow a process similar to the installation of any other fun-for-the-whole-family entertainment draw. Touring circuses, after all, were already more than a century deep in the cultural consciousness.

Malls-as-zoos elicit a feel-bad feeling similar to a GoFundMe for someone's life-saving medical treatment. Like, the system is bad. We know that. But to see it displayed so overtly puts a finer point to late-capitalism distress. If putting an animal in a cage is strange, putting an animal in a cage in a *mall* is pretty perverted. It lays bare an ideology that makes no sense to me.

Our species' ability to create and conform to ideologies allows us to dominate entire ecosystems, but it doesn't mean we're more intelligent than any other form of life. I think about how trees communicate with each other through the soil, the vast networks of fungi connecting them – no human being will ever be able to speak that language. How could we possibly understand the processes that have sustained life on earth, the ancient knowledge intertwined in all of this, let alone think we're above it? So many things about life at this point in time are stupid and cruel. Making sea lions live next to an H&M feels like we're trying a little too hard to make our human short-sightedness, our human cruelty, everyone else's problem.

For this reason alone, we could say there's nothing more human than a mall. But really, if the mall has any essential quality of humanness, it's a white and colonial one, the aspects of my own identity that make this all a relatively new world view for me. To recognize malls only symbolically – pure imagination, built solely to circulate capital and things only humans care about – denies their physical and historical apparatus. It is not new to value beauty. But from a particular perspective, it is a new thing to clear living land to erect a temple to beauty; it is new to put a living being in a cage.

––––––

This is the dilemma of being a psychologically tormented horse girl. I love animals enough to ruminate over their well-being, but being in their presence is as spiritually meaningful to me as listening to a great piece of music.

You know how a singer's voice can move an inner part of you to feel like it's the one singing? At eight or nine years old, the peak of my West Edmonton Mall dolphin obsession, I experienced their grace and freedom as if those qualities belonged to me. I remember consciously suppressing tears while watching the dolphins twist through the air, waving to us with their tails, aggressive 2000s stadium-pop music echoing through the shiny space. I know this all makes me sound insane, but it was fucking moving! It was a true social experience!

The dolphins performed three times daily, which meant my family and I could catch (or they would have to drag me away from) a show every time we visited the mall. We always watched for free from the upper levels looking over the pool, though I did sit in the paid seats one time, probably because my cousins from Vancouver Island were in town. To see the dolphins' actual bellybuttons and wry smiles up close, to smell the sharp chlorinated water seeping into my running shoes, made me feel very rich, even famous. For an assignment in kindergarten, I wrote that I wanted to be a dolphin trainer when I grew up, which is beautiful in a weird way: the dolphins in the mall, for a moment in time, inspired a hope of what I, a girl with a dream in landlocked Alberta, could become without moving somewhere like Florida. I guess all children only dream of places they've already been and things they've seen people do. But I like the idea that there was a time when my future felt happily contained so close to my first home, had nothing to do with cash, and also involved sea animals.

The dolphins had been in the mall longer than I had been alive, so it never occurred to me to find their existence unordinary, let alone upsetting. I was disappointed when a mall didn't have a dolphin show. Now it's hard to see the dolphins' story as anything but depressing. The four of them, Howard, Mavis, Maria, and Gary, were intentionally captured off the coast of Florida in 1985 as five-year-olds and introduced to West Edmonton Mall in its Phase III expansion. I once thought there was something venerating about their names. Dolphins' brains are bigger than humans', and they can recognize themselves in the mirror, like chimpanzees and people – wouldn't it make sense for them to have real dignified names, also like people? It was off-putting to learn more recently that each was named after a member of the mall's managerial staff, what reads as an ironic jab at the inhumanity of dolphins: mascots for the big guys upstairs, their monikers mildly funny, like when people give their plants serious-sounding human names like Steve or Karen.

The mall also allowed the dolphins to freely breed with one another. (Which means dolphins didn't just live in the mall but had *polyamorous sex* there, too.) All five of Mavis's and Maria's babies were either stillborn or died shortly after birth. Although activists had always been quite vocal in advocating for the dolphins' release – Midnight Oil's Peter Garrett urged an Edmonton audience to rescue the 'four gentle dolphins' in 1993 – it peaked in 1996 after the third and fourth baby dolphins died in the tank within nearly a week of each other. Albertans for the Ethical Treatment of Animals, a group that had previously demonstrated outside the Ghermezians' home, staged protests at Sea Life Caverns. An outdoor-education and toy store pulled out of its lease. Naturally, anti-abortion activists joined the party, too, upset that human fetuses seemed to be getting less attention.

The discourse sparked by each event swirled in the usual ouroboros. A trainer from the new *Flipper* movie chimed in, arguing that in a dolphin's echolocative world of sound, keeping one in a tank is like committing a human to a life

sentence in a hall of mirrors. Dolphin trainers and enthusiasts retorted in the local papers that the dolphins received
top-of-the-line care, that the dolphins looked happy, and
that, anyway, the only two dolphin rehabilitation centres on
the continent, both with suspicious records of their own,
had recently closed – these hand-fed dolphins would be
shark food in the alternative reality these haters were so
thirsty for.

Throughout the whole ordeal, the mall maintained the
polished front you'd expect of any organization with a
public-relations team. When activists wrote in with their
concerns, the mall responded with a canned letter about the
threats facing dolphins in the wild and the mall's commitment to caring for their physical and emotional health,
adding that dolphins 'love people, and love to have people
appreciate them.'

The mall doubled down on its stance in August 1996,
definitively announcing to the press that they would not –
like, ever – be releasing the dolphins. A few months later, the
mall was accredited by the Canadian Association of Zoolog-
ical Parks and Aquariums (now Canada's Accredited Zoos
and Aquariums), a move that validated supporters' arguments
that the mall was a humane place to display animals, just like
any other good and normal zoo you'd visit with your family.
The decision may have even empowered the mall to consider
taking on more animals. After the mayor floated the idea of
closing the Edmonton Valley Zoo in 1997, the Ghermezians
suggested building a replacement on the mall's roof to take
in the hypothetically homeless animals. The idea ultimately
went nowhere; the Edmonton Valley Zoo still very much

exists. But you do have to admire the gall of emerging from a PR minefield and being like, 'More, please!'

Or maybe this has nothing to do with gall, but rather a startling lack of humility. Or that the thrill of getting away with something rewrites your own history; any prior threat, now free of consequence, becomes unreal. Another possibility is that the Ghermezians and other mall decision makers genuinely loved dolphins. Maybe they believed there was no better place for a once-wild animal.

Mall manager Gary Hanson did, however, give us a reason to believe otherwise. When he was making the announcement that the mall was keeping the dolphins – one of whom was named after him – he slipped in something like regret regarding the mall's decision to get them in the first place: 'Would we do it again? No, we wouldn't.'

––––––

A genuine admission of regret is dazzling. Like a car accident or a fight in public, it cuts through the stilted way we so often relate to one another: pretending we're not fuck-ups, receiving a vaguely apologetic corporate word salad and then writing the word salad ourselves, gesturing toward the bad things we've said and done and bought, only to say, do, and buy them all again.

Thrillingly, regret features in every origin story that led dolphins to live in West Edmonton Mall. Philip Henry Gosse, the inventor of institutional aquariums, expressed a lament similar to that of Victor Gruen and his 'bastard development' modern malls. The English naturalist popularized home aquariums and coined the term itself in his 1854 instructional book, *Aquarium: An Unveiling of the Wonders of the Deep Sea*, in which he advises readers to venture to the beach at low tides under a full moon, armed with a wicker basket to collect specimens. His vivid, candy-coloured illustrations of crabs, sea anemones, and kelp made the unknown – once considered terrifying – newly enchanting. The deeply religious Gosse likened studying sea creatures in his aquarium to being in the presence of God. It was the closest we could come to truly understanding something as unknowable as a higher deity's will. In his own memoir, Edmund Gosse, Philip's son, wrote that his father's books made the capturing of wild sea life more popular than he had planned. Philip felt responsible for the depletion of the English shore's rich tidal pools. He had made aquariums to make sense of a higher power, but, as Edmund lamented, the 'rough paw of well-meaning, idle-minded curiosity' destroyed the paradise Philip first admired. His intention to come closer to God was corrupted.

Malls, aquariums, aquariums in malls – the human desire to play God is consistent throughout each of them. And through examining them, it becomes clear how virtually every mundane aspect of our lives screws up the truth of how we're supposed to relate to each other. When I see malls and aquariums as unnatural, everything else defamiliarizes; my skin crawls with a sublime and sticky dread.

I hate thinking this way, as if the things that alienate us – and alienation itself – are as certain as time, as if I am somehow both the only person alive and an anonymous product of everything that's come before me.

This is why I find Gosse's, Gruen's, and Hanson's admissions a relief. Admitting to a flaw in the design means that it is a design, and in a design is the possibility that things could have been, and could also become, something different. I'm also pretty gullible. Each admission could just be the reflex of the person's own ego, distancing themself from anticipated criticism. I want to believe in genuine expressions of male vulnerability! When I think about regret as hard as I think about malls and aquariums, I lose perspective on what regret even means. Do we express regret, I wonder, to comfort the part we can't say out loud?

―――――

In 2002, Mavis gave birth to the mall's final dolphin calf, during regular shopping hours. Shoppers, including children and their alarmed parents, watched on as Mavis nudged the calf's limp body around the tank. Four, five times, she drove her nose into its body, plunging them both to the bottom before swimming back to the surface, so firmly that some bystanders thought she had killed the calf herself. (The mall's veterinarian, however, said that she may have been trying to help her calf breathe.)

Mavis never got her spark back and died one year later with no apparent cause aside from a broken heart. With Gary and Maria having died a couple of years earlier, Howard was now all alone, a plainly depressing sight: swimming listless circles, dollar-store condolence letters and flowers scattered around the tank.

Howard's declining health forced the mall to backtrack on its earlier promise to keep the dolphins forever. The

Theater of the Sea, a marine park in the Florida Keys with a 1.2-hectare saltwater lagoon, took ownership over Howard in 2004, and he lived out the rest of his days there with seven other dolphins, performing shows three times daily – but not before being escorted out of the mall in the dead of night and taking a $40,000 private flight to his new home.

Somehow, this wasn't the end of West Edmonton Mall's identity as a zoo but the beginning of a new zookeeping phase. Shortly after Mavis died, the mall acquired from the Toronto Zoo fifteen flamingos (that were replaced by eight ring-tailed lemurs in 2010). And just five months after Howard left, the mall opened its first sea lion attraction. Only three of the sea lions it had bought from a Scottish zoo made it to the mall – the fourth died on the journey over. They arrived the same way Howard left, in the middle of the night.

———

Dolphins haven't made their way back to any malls since. In Canada, they likely never will: Bill S-203, which passed in 2019, finally made it illegal to take a cetacean from the wild and display it for profit.

The fact that Edmonton had to be the place for this whole ordeal to shake out is poetic. For one, my hometown has a thing for controversially holding animals captive. At times, Lucy, an Indian elephant living at the Edmonton Valley Zoo, has been the city's best-known resident. She has lived alone since 2007, after her companion of eighteen years was moved to another zoo, and former *Price Is Right* game-show host Bob Barker made freeing the elephant the final crusade of his public life. After he offered $100,000 to buy Lucy outright, the mayor at the time retaliated by suggesting that Barker get a real job to occupy himself and leave Edmonton alone. Just like the dolphins, Lucy was and still is apparently too old and ill to endure the journey to a better place.

This fuck-off, sunk-cost fallacy has everything and nothing to do with Edmonton. How many things do we all do that we know are bad but continue doing anyway? The energy becomes more pointed in a place so geographically and culturally close to where people still get rich from yanking oil from the ground, a place where the biggest mall lives for them to spend all this money. Not to mention a place where people put metal testicles on their trucks. I've also watched enough *Tiger King* and been around enough oddball horse people – a chronic insecurity lurks under the bravado of people who insist upon holding a wild animal captive. The insecurity becomes apparent when people desperately justify that captivity, publicly, for decades.

It does not help that Calgary, Edmonton's enemy in all things, has a nice and reputable zoo that's twice the size of Edmonton's. *Edmonton Journal* columnist Tim Mikula phrased it best when he drew a comparison between Edmonton's inferiority complex, the dolphins, the elephant, and the mediocre Oilers' hostage-holding of all-star hockey player Connor McDavid: 'We're a city so blinded by our own self-congratulatory boosterism we'll do anything to anyone to prove to the world that despite being mostly composed of parking lots, we're a World Class City. In practice this means forcing animals to live in a mall and ruining a generational talent.'

I don't mind the fact that Edmonton has this chip on its shoulder. It makes my hometown (and me, by extension) more interesting. Knowing you're a bit shitty but never admitting it, and unsuccessfully trying to prove otherwise, has a more literary quality than being merely good or merely bad. The tension gives us texture, something to talk about.

But this quality must extend beyond Edmonton. The flyover cities and roadside attractions of the world that love their miserable animals can't stop talking about their miserable animals. Lovingly squeezing the life out of some silent creature puts us on the map.

And who can't relate? We are all mall dolphins; we are all malls. None of us can escape where we've come from; we can't let precious things go.

———

Recently, a group of seven-year-old students at a school in England finished a class study on *The One and Only Ivan*. They then wrote short paragraphs from the perspective of the gorilla after he was released into Zoo Atlanta. Each captures the triumph of the moment; some demonstrate a surprising understanding of trauma and memory – Ivan can't quite trust that he is free at last.

'I run around in worry thinking someone would take this freedom away,' reads one of the pieces. 'But after a minute I realize it is fine. I think this is my reality. I am free.'

The real story isn't nearly this cathartic. By the time Ivan died at Zoo Atlanta, after eighteen years of living there, he hadn't made close bonds with any other gorillas at the Ford

African Rain Forest. Local newspapers published, in increasingly frustrated tones, articles about Ivan's lack of interest in mating before eventually dropping the topic altogether.

I don't know if this chapter of his life made Ivan happy or sad, or if gorillas feel happiness and sadness in the same way I do. The experience of living alone inside a mall for most of one's life must pervert one's perception of either. What is freedom, after that – to a person, to a gorilla?

The clearest truth about Ivan's story is the feeling it produces. *The One and Only Ivan* uses as its epigraph a quote attributed to George Eliot: 'It is never too late to be what you might have been.' In her acceptance speech for the Newbery Award, Katherine Applegate mused on the similarities among Eliot, who assumed a male pseudonym to work as a writer in the Victorian era; Applegate herself, who wrote her first book in her fifties; and Ivan, having, I guess, realized his potential as a gorilla later in life. She did acknowledge the real Ivan's imperfect ending. He was still in a cage, but now he was surrounded by people and animals who cared for him. Ultimately, Applegate's speech landed on children's abilities to conceptualize sadness. The job of a children's book writer, she said, is to harness their imaginations and show them joy and wonder, a pre-emptive or curative way to cope with the inevitable sadness of life.

Much the same could be said for animals. They educate us in what's soft, innate, and often unknown; they mirror some universal experience of feeling trapped by circumstances beyond our control or understanding.

For better or for worse, our stories about animals in captivity will always reveal more about the person telling the story than about the animal itself. In a recent article about a miserable-looking zoo in a Minnesota mall, for example, one employee talks about how she came to the job needing a change of pace from her previous one at a hospital, where she had treated victims of shootings, stabbings, and overdoses. She said her job at the zoo was the best one she's ever had – animals, she added, are much nicer than people.

I would say something cynical about this, but then I remember a line from a letter to the editor published in the *Edmonton Journal* in 1993: 'As seniors on fixed income, one of our pleasures is a walk through West Edmonton Mall and a visit with the dolphins.'

Or there's Jennifer Fouts, a twenty-three-year-old cancer survivor who made the news for swimming with the dolphins in 1986. She told the paper that it had been the greatest dream of her life. 'There's no other way to describe it. In all my life I never thought I'd get a chance to do something like this,' she said at the mall, months before dying unexpectedly after receiving a heart transplant.

A former mall employee wrote in to the paper to argue that the dolphins were not only perfectly healthy in their enclosure but spoiled brats. But, he wrote, 'when you look into their eyes there is a communication which I am unable to explain except to say that it generates a feeling of well-being.'

This isn't exactly what Gruen was going for when he first elected to have animals in the very first mall. Animals were installed in the original mall to facilitate a more enticing shopping experience, not quite the transcendent experience documented here of making eye contact, and what we can only hope is a true connection with another being through the glass. No part of me would want to suggest that this makes the whole history of animals in malls somehow worth it. It is, however, an important feature of the story. Zoos, malls, capitalism: they all represent some endeavour to capture what's beyond the borders of our understanding. It's awe-inspiring; it's so sad.

Having an affinity for animals that stops short of actual liberation isn't the same thing as empathy. The way we love or grieve something reflects the degree to which it belongs to us, and us to them.

———

The first thing I ever wrote about the mall, which was also the earliest version of this book chapter, was an essay about the animals inside of it. The essay about mall animals ended up being an essay about everything: Gruen's and Gosse's regret, being a weird and difficult kid who liked horses, feeling trapped in the way that animals in zoos might. It was about grieving the death of my friend who had recently been struck and killed by a train. It was about going to the mall aquarium because I find aquariums relaxing, a problematic idea as a vegan who should know better. If I could pick one thing the essay was about, it would be the way that grief turns everything into a metaphor of itself.

Reading the essay now, I notice the lengths I go to explain myself. The star regret, it turns out, isn't Gruen's or Gosse's. It's mine. There's a whole paragraph on 'the physical barriers between me and the things I will not do on principle': eating meat, getting single-use to-go cups from coffee shops, exerting the control I want over my own life, the control I want over the environment. I write with guilty attachment about being awestruck by a sea turtle gracefully swimming in a tank; I then wonder if all my behaviours are somehow protecting an abstract version of the turtle, its far-off ancestral relatives in the real ocean. I seem to be tiptoeing around the real idea that must have been too revealing to put to words at the time: my desire to protect and enjoy the things I care about ends up harming them; my desire to protect myself must harm me, too.

Publishing my writing, recording my thoughts as if I have resolved them, is so dishonest. I find it shocking, for example, how I published that essay while leaving out the part that has eaten me alive: I had left my friend on read for days, only responding to his text unknowingly minutes after his death. This moment affirmed the deepest truth I believe about myself, which is that I am a bad person. Not just morally, but functionally. For someone so desperate for connection, I am physically incapable of returning a message on time. And, because I'm an idiot, I have never considered there would be a consequence to being this way, at least not to the tune of someone being gone forever before knowing they were important to me. I could have left this part out of the essay on purpose. The truth could have dawned on me in the years since writing the essay. True to form, I cannot remember.

My greatest, longest aspiration has been to be good. When my therapist asked me how old that feeling was, I was like, 'Since the dawn of time.'

I wonder if that's why I was drawn to writing in the first place: to articulate who I want to be. I would like to tell people precisely how they should understand me. At the beginning of the COVID-19 pandemic, I wrote a kind of insane op-ed in the *Globe and Mail* saying that people shouldn't fly in planes anymore. It has resulted in more than one awkward interaction where mentioning that I took a plane ride felt like admitting to being a hypocrite, when really all I was trying to say in the article was that I wanted the world to slow down.

This happens all the time: I accidentally let slip how flimsy my rules are, and any moral shield I've projected about myself is revealed to be as flimsy as I am. Like, the other day, I ate an oyster for the first time. It was a sunny day on a patio; I wanted to finally see what the big deal was. In truth, I wanted to detach from the rigid rules I've made for myself, which I can better understand now as a crutch or protection against losing control. I don't quite remember what the oyster tasted like, aside from salt water. (I think that's the whole point of oysters.) I don't think the experience was worth another creature losing its life, but I also don't know the extent to which oysters live life. My greatest regret is doing it around other people. My partner later let my transgression slip to a friend of ours, a more hardcore vegan, and I wanted to die. His speaking it into existence meant that the oyster had happened; it became a fact about myself.

In the mall, I cannot ignore my desire for goodness, for restriction. I am presented with everything I want and everything I have done to stop myself from experiencing pleasure; this makes it both satisfying and exhausting when I break these rules. I think fast fashion is inhumane and it's ruining the planet, so I'll spend a truly absurd amount of time and money making a linen dress by hand in my bedroom. And then suddenly I am trying on a thirty-dollar bra that holds me so well it could be a spiritual experience. I don't feel like a good person when I buy it. To be honest, though, I don't feel like a good person when I am making a linen dress, either. I'm sure I would feel the same if I were truly saving the world; I'd feel the same if I were living in a hole.

Creating restrictions around myself has given me a sense of narrative agency when I have felt as though the world is eating me alive. Putting an arc to my actions is confirmation that I exist, much like putting an animal in a cage is a narrative act, and putting an animal in a cage in a mall is a similar yet separate one.

———

The quietest place in West Edmonton Mall is inside the famous bronze whale. Only a few people can fit inside at a time. It's completely dark, except for an eerie red light in the place where its whale uvula must be. It smells salty and warm, like blood or pennies held in a palm. When I was a kid in Sunday school, the bronze whale was my analogue for Jonah's three days and three nights alone in the belly of the whale: dark and womblike, gently dulling the harsh edges of the music and sins and mistakes on the outside.

The whale was controversially moved to storage to make a seating area for husbands and boyfriends outside the new Victoria's Secret. After five years, the mall brought it out of storage and reinstalled it in one of the less popular areas of the mall, before moving it again to make way for a new Toyota dealership. It's the same whale as before, but it no longer lives in the pool of water it lived in when I was a child. The same but different. As a result, I feel old.

Everyone I know from Edmonton speaks fondly about the whale, usually with an excited tone of irony. Of course our mall has a weird and giant whale, among all the other weird and giant things about it. Everyone calls it The Whale, but it has an actual name – *Open Sea* – and creation story.

The mall commissioned Robin Bell, a Canadian sculptor living in Italy, to make it. He decided to model the whale on the actual dimensions of a right whale, using the measurements of a hundred-year-old right whale skull at the University of Pisa. The sculpture has a feature that allows it to blow water out of its spout, which the mall has never utilized, to Bell's disappointment. He chose this particular whale for two reasons: it is found on both Canadian coasts and it is one of the most endangered whale species. I think this fact is important. It means there is a subtext of urgency to this seemingly random artifact of the mall and of my life. This thing of which I have only a self-centred understanding has a silent political story. I never would have conceived of it as a site of protest.

Right whales have crept closer to extinction every year since Bell finished his sculpture. Activists trying to save the last of them are up against fishing lines and Maine's billion-dollar lobster industry. I've heard enough stories in my life to know there are two ways this could end.

Here's one way: the bronze whale in the mall will outlive the real ones in the ocean. There is a very real possibility that in the future, someone could look at this whale and the barnacles on its face and the readable kindness in its metal eyes and know that this is the realest it gets. They could imagine the real whale it was modelled upon; they could imagine the hundreds that were like it. They could imagine the ocean, past or present. It's possible they could think about the person who made the bronze whale and how hopeful that person must have been, how much he must have loved life to make something in its image.

Accidents

Big things don't make sense. In general, human minds are bad at creating a meaningful understanding between ourselves and things that are larger than we are: numbers, deaths, histories, malls.

You can think about how this played out in the COVID-19 pandemic, when news of six-million-and-climbing deaths may have washed over your head, as it did mine, like a conceptually unsettling but truly inconceivable mist. This response, often referred to as 'psychic numbing,' is irrational: the distress we feel about one individual stranger's suffering does not magnify, but rather detaches, when we try to conjure the hundreds, thousands, millions just like them. In the news, academics have chalked this up to evolutionarily baked-in flaws, namely the human brain's inability to conceptualize large numbers. They often cite a 2013 study in which half its participants, when instructed to arrange large numbers on a linear plane, placed one million about halfway between one thousand and one billion. If you were to correctly draw it out, one million would be one thousand times closer to one thousand, nuzzled up all the way on the left-hand side. Telling the public about a colossal death toll, then, is rarely enough to incite meaningful personal change. We can't see ourselves in relation to it.

This should be embarrassing, but the clearest takeaway from this news, for me, is a sense of comfort: I'm not alone in my self-centred understanding of scale. More tangibly, it must mean I'm not the only one who regularly feels unmoored by numbers and everything they represent. Not just the disastrously large ones, but the small ones, too. This is never more evident than when I'm shopping. I'll buy a forty-dollar shirt because it's ten dollars cheaper than a fifty-dollar one. But the more expensive something gets, the less weight I give the numbers; ignoring the boots on sale, I won't blink at spending an extra fifty dollars for the boots my heart desires. I feel like a morally bad person for spending eight dollars on a latte, and just inadvertently racked up seventy-eight dollars on my credit card at the dollar store because when something costs ninety-nine cents, my brain registers it as being free. I then mount all this on my more foundational belief: that my inability to understand how money works is the actual reason I'll never not live paycheque to paycheque, the actual reason I can't see myself affording my life in the future, which is the actual reason why my life in the present occasionally doesn't feel real. I can snap out of it and convince myself that this isn't the case. But the shame is persistent, more raw or true than any number.

———

According to enough guys in my undergrad poli-sci classes, about 100 million people died as a result of communism in the Soviet Union. I've never been sure how true that is. But it's a pretty genius way to shut down a conversation that's inching toward an argument that favours socialism. I can't begin to question how one would calculate this number, or argue to what extent the Soviet Union was *actually* communist, let alone wonder if it's a small or large death toll compared to capitalism's, without coming across as somewhat chill about a large number of people dying.

Even if we were to lob that counter-argument, everyone's calculation of capitalism's death toll would shake out differently. For example, does every death in a mall count as a death by capitalism? Every overdose? Every death as a result of a war that had more than a little bit to do with oil? And isn't that basically all wars?

I feel fairly certain that Rana Plaza, an eight-storey factory in Bangladesh that made clothes for North American and European fast-fashion retailers, could only have existed in an economic system that prioritizes private property and profit. I feel less certain around who's to blame for the factory's collapse in 2013, which killed 1,134 of its workers. Up until the moment it fell, workers were forced to continue showing up despite obvious cracks forming on the inside of the building. To blame capitalism for their deaths seems as meaningless as attributing it all to an act of God. But then again, I struggle to extricate the individual greed that made Rana Plaza dangerous in the first place from the economic system we live under. Disregarding human life seems so integral to business operating as usual that I find myself assuming this building's existence was somewhat natural, so inevitable that its collapse *could* pass as an act of God.

The amorphousness of calculating all this borders on pointlessness – and not because people can't grasp large numbers. In any situation, a death toll becomes meaningful only when it intersects with our own personal and cultural definitions of a valuable life. Like this: when I read the number of how many people died at Rana Plaza, my mind reflexively counted it as half a 9/11. Weirdly, I don't remember where I was on September 11, 2001, but I do remember the days and weeks after it, namely learning that approximately three thousand people died. Three thousand, I assumed, was the relative number it took for something to become a big deal. Obviously, it wasn't the number of people who died that incited a war and the fact that we still have to put our liquids in a plastic baggie at the airport, but it is just one example of how the most important death is one that borders on your own.

———

On June 14, 1986, only six months after West Edmonton Mall's Mindbender roller coaster opened to the public, the rear car crashed, sending its four passengers flying into a concrete pillar and the floor below, killing three of them and shattering the legs, pelvis, and ribs of the fourth.

The crash's mythology has hung over Edmonton ever since; the details have only gotten muddier over time. Growing up, I knew that the Mindbender crashed before I was born, but I was unsure of much else – how it crashed, how many died – aside from the fact that the roller coaster was a killer. More than one person I've spoken to has insisted that it happened after a sweater thrown onto the tracks got tangled in the roller coaster's wheels.

What everyone does seem to know, however, is where they or their families were that day. They were at the water-park, their cousin was in line to board then decided against it, their dad saw it happen. I think my aunt was there that night, or had wanted to go that night, or something. What's more fascinating than this: your own interaction with not only a spectacular piece of local history, but the event that could have vaporized your existence, or the possibility of your future existence, all in an unlucky instant. These stories are, tragically, boring to everyone else, about as interesting as hearing where someone's dad went for lunch on a weekday thirty-five years ago.

As a result, the Mindbender is a pretty tiresome mascot of Edmonton's local imagination. In 2023, when the mall announced that it would finally demolish the roller coaster, I couldn't help but feel relieved. Surely nobody liked the actual experience of the Mindbender; with one of the highest G-forces of any roller coaster in the world, it wasn't fun to ride, but a test of endurance. I hated the scream of the Mind-bender's wheels on the tracks, how it filled Galaxyland with the harshest sound, like a metal zipper splitting your skull in half. Even when it wasn't running, which seemed like most of the time, the looming, carcass-like structure filled me with dread, the same dark feeling of looking into a construction zone at night. I do wonder, though, if this is only because of what I know, what I have always known, about the Mind-bender – if my hatred of the roller coaster was an abstract and narcissistic fear that it could kill me, too.

My top-tier fears involve being hurt or killed in public. Half of the fear, if I could measure it, has to do with my lack of agency in preventing things from happening. I can't trust that people will always stop at red lights at an intersection, for example, instead of plowing into my car. I'm worried about where I'd go if the west coast's devastating, overdue earthquake hits while I'm downtown and surrounded by falling glass windows. I also dread the idea of being vulnerable around people I hardly know. If I am unconscious around strangers, how will I know if they mistreat me?

One of the worst things about dying in public is that it becomes other people's business. They see it, they read about it, they talk about it – the most personal thing you go through becomes something everyone can spin meaning from: a lesson to stave off their own mortality, a piece of evidence toward a cultural critique. I learned this the day after my friend was killed in public; he was out for a run before work when he was struck by an LRT near the university. In the comments section below a news story about the event, with what I can only describe as righteous anger, several people chalked it up as a cautionary tale about the dangers of wearing headphones in public and the carelessness of young adults. The tragedy was proof that they were right, about whatever, all along.

You'd be hard-pressed to find a more culturally significant place to be hurt than a mall. An injury in a place like this turns an invisible anxiety – the danger of materialism, youth, strangers – into something felt in the body, suddenly real.

And if the potential violence of malls could be contained in a day, it would be Black Friday. The anonymously run black-fridaydeathcount.com tallied all publicly reported injuries and deaths at Black Friday sales from 2006 to 2021. It lists seventeen deaths and 125 injuries, including a couple of predictable portraits of American mayhem: an employee trampled to death by a throng of two hundred shoppers, an off-duty police officer pepper-spraying twenty rowdy shoppers at a Walmart. But it also includes examples of violence and tragedy that have hardly anything to do with shoppers clamouring over each other for a deal. A trans woman was viciously attacked one Black Friday at a Kohl's; another year, an exhausted early-morning shopper fell asleep at the wheel and crashed, killing two of his daughters in the back seat.

A couple of years ago, someone shared the Black Friday Death Count on Reddit. The top comment, up-voted more than one thousand times, admits that 'for some reason, I thought it would be more extreme' – somehow, the real violence of this day isn't large enough to cradle its symbolic weight. Black Friday should be more violent than it is.

Morbidly, I had a similar experience while looking for examples of death and injury at West Edmonton Mall. I was surprised to learn that 'only' one murder has happened there. In 1996, a nineteen-year-old was stabbed in a gang-related attack on Boxing Day. Any death is significant, especially for the people closest to it. Still, West Edmonton Mall's actual history of violence doesn't reflect my imagining of it.

I guess I was expecting to find more evidence of how the material fantasy of this uniquely huge mall motivates people to do uniquely bad things. To be honest, I don't know what I expected these uniquely bad things to be. Someone getting so turnt on Bath & Body Works sales that they choked someone? Does the spirit of the Gruen transfer, that psychological state that makes us shop carelessly, also unhinge our moral compass to the point of permitting murder? Imagining this is fascinating in the same way I find the Wikipedia pages about Disneyland and Disney World deaths fascinating. People losing limbs and life on something as banal as the PeopleMover dramatically cuts through the happy fantasy of the place. These stories also undercut anything I tell myself (or friends or small children) in order to override my human instinct to avoid danger and climb aboard a machine specifically designed to make me feel like I'm on the brink of death.

Realistically, West Edmonton Mall features as a dizzying symbolic backdrop to crimes people were already committing. In 2007, for example, a teenager was hired to kill a local drug dealer. After finishing his hit, he went on a shopping spree, buying a BlackBerry, new shoes, a watch, and a $9.50 novelty beer-straw hat. He then rented the Hollywood suite at the Fantasyland Hotel with his friend, where they took pictures of themselves stuffing cash into their mouths. More recently, a woman took her three children on a shopping spree and a trip to Galaxyland the day before she unsuccessfully attempted to kill herself and them in a house fire, her intent made apparent by a suicide note she wrote on Fantasyland Hotel stationery. The incriminating note factored into her sentencing to ten years in prison.

If you stretch your imagination a bit, the anonymity offered by the crowded public space could be considered an accomplice in some cases, like when Jayme Pasieka went to the mall's military supply store to buy the two knives he used to stab six and kill two of his co-workers at a grocery warehouse. In this sense, the mall has sometimes operated as a medium for people to temporarily pass through undetected. On a day pass at the mall for his birthday, an inmate serving time for murder overpowered an unarmed guard. He spent fifty-two days on the lam, during which he killed two people. In 2004, a man was reported missing after his truck was found abandoned in the mall parking lot. A year and a half later, his best friend was charged with his murder. Later, the friend admitted that he had planned to dump the truck at the airport but didn't have enough cash to take a cab back into the city.

Most violence at West Edmonton Mall has been accidental, seemingly inflicted by the structure of the building itself. A woman snagged and degloved her finger on the Corkscrew waterslide, for example. Several men have been injured from jumping into the lagoon, and two have died in it: one drowned during a drunk swim; the other, a scuba diver, got tangled in an air pump after doing maintenance on one of the submarines. The height of the mall seems to be the most dangerous thing about it. In 2003, a young man accepted a dare from a friend to leap from the second floor; he later died of the injuries he sustained by striking his head on a Canada Post kiosk. People fall from escalators and the parkade; a painter died after falling off his scaffolding in Europa Boulevard; kids tumble over guardrails and, miraculously, most of the time, survive.

But more often than that, West Edmonton Mall is just there when bad things, the most banal or banally tragic moments in people's lives, happen. Once, a teenage father claimed his daughter had been abducted from his truck in the mall parking lot before it was revealed that she had died of sudden infant death syndrome; he had left her body wrapped in blankets where he hoped nobody would find her, in a wooded area fifty kilometres south of the city. The theme of that story, I think, is shame. But I can't think of anything meaningful to say about the others, the several elderly people who were struck by cars on their way to the mall: one about to return a purchase at Sears, another to pick up insulin for his wife. I think of a mother who waited forty-five minutes for her daughter to show up for lunch on Bourbon Street, before worrying and driving into the city to find her. Eventually, she came upon her daughter's crushed vehicle and body, as if she had predicted the accident herself.

————

In a 2016 essay for the *New Inquiry*, Erik Forman recalls the bleak six years he spent working in the Mall of America's rotunda as a Starbucks barista. One weekend, the rotunda hosted a competition in which six contestants chained themselves to a suitcase of cash, in hopes they could outlast the others and take home a grand prize of $10,000. As Forman considered the parallels between the competition and his own plight, chained to making poverty wages with no clear way out, he heard a sickening thud. A person had jumped to their death from the upper levels of the mall. In the hour that passed, he watched paramedics wheel the body away and janitors clean the person's blood from the floor. Within the same shift, shoppers walked over the very spot as if nothing had happened. Once again, Forman saw a metaphor form before his eyes. As bodies broke and bled around it, the mall itself remained immortally pristine, impermeable.

Malls are not a particularly popular place for people to die by suicide. Mall suicides are, however, particularly strange. Despite being overtly public acts – seen and heard by dozens of strangers in close range – they are hardly ever immortalized in the public record. North American and European news outlets rarely report on suicides; the standard logic seems to be that reporting on the details could inspire copycats.

In a *Maisonneuve* essay, Fawn Parker writes about witnessing a man jump to his death in Toronto's Eaton Centre. She tries, several times, to find an article or a social media post about the event she has surely just seen. All that turns up is an article written a couple of years earlier about someone taking their life in the exact same place in the exact same way – as if the thing she just saw had never happened. Or as if it has never stopped and will never stop happening. 'How many others,' she writes, 'have been erased from the mall?'

Unless you've witnessed it yourself, you'll probably only hear about a mall suicide if it's taken on meaning as something else, if the significance has rippled out widely enough to become more topical than an individual's decision to cease existing (or important enough to risk the chance of it happening again?). For example, the four suicide attempts, including two successful ones, at West Edmonton Mall's shooting range made national news. The stories, however, focused very little on the events and people themselves. The greater narrative touched on the existence of gun ranges, their potential for violence, the question of whether events like this could be prevented in the future.

In other cases, mall suicides make the news because of how other people have responded to them. In 2023, for example, a Parisian man's death made the news when shoppers mistook the sound of his body hitting the ground for a gunshot, inciting a mass-panic stampede. One of the more viral stories of mall suicide happened at Golden Eagle International Shopping Center in Xuzhou, China. Witnesses claimed that the man jumped to his death after becoming fed up with his girlfriend's demands to continue shopping. Published in outlets like Gawker and the *Daily News*, the story doesn't feel newsworthy. It feels like a punchline, an ironic gesture of solidarity with guys with wives worldwide.

Malls, then, evade the literary fortitude of culturally signifi-cant suicide spots, such as Japan's Aokigahara Forest or the Golden Gate Bridge. Mall suicides may not loom large in stat-ure or memory, but do, frustratingly, in the minds of people who have come close to these deaths.

In a piece for *Salon*, Eric Van Hoose wrestles with making meaning out of mall violence. Pulling the thread on his local mall, Destiny USA in Syracuse, New York, revealed that at least three people had plunged to their deaths from the six-storey atrium. Published one month after terrorist attacks at Kenya's Westgate Mall killed seventy-one people, the article probes why violence happens in malls in the first place. Van Hoose argues that violence is not just symbolized at the mall but actively reproduced there, a feature rather than a bug: the exploitation of low-wage workers, all circulating goods often made by even more exploited workers on the other side of the world. And it isn't a stretch, he writes, to consider that someone's deep sadness, loneliness, or hopelessness could become more acute in the mall. When you're broke, the fantasy projected by storefronts is a cruel one.

I do realize that there's an impossibility, or even disrespect of an individual's internal life, in attempting to make meaning of any suicide, inside the mall or out. I learned about this from my favourite podcast, one in which two therapists record an hour-long session with someone who has written in asking for advice. In one episode, a woman was processing her father's suicide, namely the fact that her mother had blamed her for his choice to end his life. One of the therapists reassured her that suicide is an intensely personal act — making reason out of the decision is as impossible as crawling into a dead person's head. The only thing we can ever know about a person's choice to end their life, she said, is that they chose to do it. The same could be said for making sense of someone making this particular choice inside a shopping mall. Homogenizing the true incomprehensibility of someone's inner life with the greater arc of late capitalism can't possibly tell the whole story.

Still, I don't think any qualified therapist would deny the vast external influence of structural violence on mental illness, how racism and poverty and other forms of discriminatory violence compel someone to make a decision that they would not have made in an alternatively structured universe. And I can't linger on the idea of choice without considering how much our choices are bound to aspects beyond ourselves. I can't think of choice, either, without thinking about when I have considered the choice myself. I no longer wanted to be me. But the other, larger part was that I no longer wanted to be me, here.

————

I was in a mall food court when my mind first became a liability to me. I was thirteen when it happened: the space between life and death thinned out, and I told my mom, across a tray of A&W, that I couldn't breathe. I know it would be more accurate to call this my first panic attack, but that hardly captures how this event reconceptualized my experience of being alive; it triggered a decade of compulsions around my fear, which later became what bordered on a prophetic understanding, that my death was coming soon and that I could play a role in preventing it. I still hesitate to label any of this as mental illness, as if labelling it as such would deny how real it felt to me. And yet (of course) the only thing that made it go away was treating it like any other physical condition of the body.

I'm sure my mind has always been a liability to me – I just became aware of it in the food court. The more I learn about my family history, the more my brain being the way it is seems inevitable. And I can't help but think things would have turned out differently if anyone in my lineage had been rich, as if my genetics are indistinguishable from my family members' trauma, as if my family members' trauma is indistinguishable from the constraints of life in the working class. And this brings me back to a core belief of mine: my life would be different if money wasn't real, which must mean some essential part of me exists because of money. But who can say where a disease begins and ends? In a brain? In a family tree? My theory could be bullshit. My theory could be nothing but an utterance of my elemental desire, presently and historically, for *more*.

Unfortunately, I can't remember a time before I cared about possessions. In my earliest memory, I am three years old and pissed: standing alone in my family's basement, holding a screwdriver, stabbing the shit out of an inflatable ball pit my parents got my sister for her second birthday. I was oblivious to the fact that they thought it would be a nice thing for all three of their kids – me, my sister, and our baby brother – to have. I wish this weren't the case, but the strongest feeling I associate with childhood is a raw, wrathful jealousy. Completely devastated when my first cousin was born and my grandma moved in with my aunt, I was later an emotional wreck when that cousin's pet guinea pig unexpectedly had a baby. I was tortured by the idea that I would never be so lucky. On my brother's first birthday, I couldn't stand the spread of gift bags laid before him, the circle of fawning adults helping him unearth the presents from beneath the tissue paper. I walked into the pantry, stripped naked, tore open a bag of flour, and dumped it over my head. I then paraded myself around the kitchen, silently begging anyone to delight in me, to be angry with me, to look at me. In my mind, this is who I am at my very core: convinced that I'm not getting my fair share, obsessed with making it everyone else's problem.

Here, I feel obligated to list every element that makes writing this hurtful to my parents and how I was, indeed, privileged as a child. My parents shelled out all the time and money to fulfill my white-girl destiny of horseback riding

lessons and dance classes. Disneyland, braces. Embarrassingly, fascinatingly, I was still jealous of my friends whose
dads spent two-thirds of the month up north, the same ones
who eventually got two Christmases after their parents got
divorced, then got free cars and didn't have to work and spent
the weekends studying because their parents paid their
tuition. This dark hole inside of myself, convinced that I
would be better if I had a little bit more, feeling like an alien
in a world that was completely built for me.

And yet! It was a revelatory moment when my favourite
political theory professor, while reading Žižek, bestowed our
seminar with the line that 'it's easier to imagine the end of
the world than the end of capitalism.' By this point, I had
established the economic system as everything that was
wrong with the world: the prison industrial complex, animal
cruelty, my maxed-out credit card, and the hours I, being
carless in St. Albert, spent trapped with my own thoughts
on the bus to and from campus. The structures informing
seemingly every aspect of my life, the planet's life, felt inevitable and painful. I felt the same way about myself: unable to
untangle the moment I became rotten, to what extent my
rottenness was socially constructed.

And so this end-of-the-world quote instilled a great degree
of hope in me, though I don't think it was ever meant to be
hopeful. The idea of *imagination*, however, suggested that a
different world was out there and that it was my job to invent
or manifest it with my mind. The quote had also been
attributed to so many different people that I came to believe
the sentiment belonged to all of us. Now it has been circulated
so often that it's basically become a meme.

The phrase returned to me in 2016, when I was working my first full-time office job after graduating university and moving to Vancouver. I spent what felt like entire months toggling between Outlook tabs and Twitter, spawning a concerning number of miserable tweets poorly disguised as half-baked cultural criticism. I experienced boredom as if it were physical torture; I interacted with millionaire philanthropists and their keepers on a daily basis, which felt like a personal affront to my condition. I hated that I spent more time pretending to look productive than I did actually working. Most of all, I hated that this all felt inevitable if I wanted to continue paying rent in #latecapitalism. All my friends lived somewhere else. Hillary Clinton lost the U.S. presidential election, which fractured a fundamental structure of my world view in more ways than I'd like to admit. I was straight-up losing my marbles and being publicly annoying about it. See also: I was twenty-two years old.

This was when Mark Fisher's writing had suddenly appeared all over my timeline. I learned that he had famously put the 'it's easier to imagine' phrase into writing in *Capitalist Realism*, a book that, in short, untangled the cultural mechanisms that make global capitalism feel like an inevitability – to the extent that a lot of us don't put much conscious thought to the economic system at all. Fisher's ideas kept me company at a time when I felt physically and ideologically isolated, now slightly less insane for feeling as if I had seen through the critical theory matrix.

It was the most ignorant phase of my life. I hadn't even bothered to wonder why Fisher's ideas had appeared all over my internet in the first place. Eventually, I learned that he had recently died by suicide. This news confronted me with a new idea: the one world you can imagine ending is your own.

———

In the years following her son's death, Annette LeSueur began walking the Mall of America alone. It was her last resort. She had petitioned the city and the mall to erect safety barriers in the atrium and parkade, but after her calls went unanswered, she made herself a wearable sandwich board that would render the banal backdrop of the mall sinister in relief. Your eye is first drawn to a photo of her son as a little boy before taking in the rest of it: a smaller image of the parkade he had leapt from, arresting yellow text reading 'NO MORE SUICIDES AT MALL OF AMERICA.'

LeSueur's story highlights the common ideological and bureaucratic stalemate concerning suicide barriers' place in malls. As long as the building is up to code, a local government doesn't have much authority to compel a mall to install them. In Syracuse, a city councillor once tried to pass a bill requiring the Destiny USA mall to install safety barriers after falling bodies and objects had injured children in the food court. Council was ultimately dissuaded by the state, since changes to building codes could complicate real estate development in the area. For decades, people have made similar demands at Palisades Center mall in New York's Rockland County, where at least seven people have ended their lives. The widower of a woman who died there filed an ultimately unsuccessful personal injury case against the mall in 2022. Now on the brink of bankruptcy, Palisades Center is more likely to close its doors than install any meaningful structural barriers.

Suicide barriers work. Toronto's Bloor Viaduct used to be one of North America's most-frequented spots for people to end their lives, second only to the Golden Gate Bridge. Installing the 'Luminous Veil' barrier in 2003 virtually ended all deaths at the spot, and in the following years, suicide rates decreased across the city by other means as well. These structures are, nevertheless, a famously hard sell. People in San Francisco, for example, have been calling for the city to install nets on the Golden Gate Bridge since the 1950s; the city didn't approve funding for them until 2014, and construction is expected to run until 2026. Confoundingly, many new structures aren't built with this liability in mind. People have been jumping off the Vessel, the sixteen-storey observation tower tacked onto the side of the Hudson Yards shopping complex, ever since it opened in 2019. With no evident solution, the $200 million tower closed to the public indefinitely for the second time, in August 2021. To build something so tall and not expect someone to jump is an act of wilful ignorance – materializing the wish that death can't happen in a place where it doesn't belong. Barriers, not unlike memorials, are physical reminders of a space's history and active potential as a place where people die.

Malls aren't favourable to memorials, either. Rodney Chayko, the survivor of the crashed Mindbender car at West Edmonton Mall, has tried and failed to get the mall to install some acknowledgement of the event, like a memorial bench, in Galaxyland. He says that mall management has suggested putting a memorial plaque in an administrative office instead. This, of course, would defeat the purpose. He doesn't need the mall staff, but everyone else, to remember the crash. So in interviews with the media, when another anniversary of the crash comes around, Chayko wears a hoodie screen-printed with the names of the three victims, 'Always in our hearts' written in white script above.

To be fair, the bench probably would have been a bummer. And although barriers on tall bridges are good, humane things, I'm never particularly thrilled to see one, to be reminded of how we fail each other while craning my wrist through the iron slats of a fence to take an increasingly pointless-feeling picture of a sunset. It wouldn't feel any different, if not more psychically pointed, in a mall. I go to the mall when I want to forget my human form and the responsibilities that come with it. In a mall, I will never be in the right frame of mind to receive a memorial. Are we so irony-poisoned that it would only read as funny – funny in a bad way, but still funny?

Mall memorials, for better or for worse, just don't compute. A mall is one of the few places that makes self-invention literal, visible, and even moderately accessible. Multiply that by the mall's number of stores, the majority of which we will never enter, and our individual possibility feels essentially infinite: the mall contains more potential forms of me than even I can picture. If we conceive of ourselves as matter – and draw our value from how our matter looks and feels – the mall is life-giving. And if we conceive of ourselves as matter, death is inconceivable, catastrophic. If the whole point of our being here is to be *something*, how can we ever reconcile becoming nothing?

'This is terror,' anthropologist Ernest Becker wrote in *The Denial of Death*. 'To have emerged from nothing, to have a name, consciousness of self, deep inner feelings, an excruciating inner yearning for life and self-expression – and with all this yet to die.'

Logic should follow that death is anathema to the whole project of shopping and the malls we do it in. Any overt reminder of our mortality would more likely propel us into an existential spiral – that is, an even more devastating existential spiral than the one you might normally find in the change rooms at Zara or looking for a parking spot on Boxing Day. Not a spirit that would inspire people to spend money. If we became pointedly aware of our mortality in a mall, wouldn't we rather head home and spend the time we have left with our friends and families?

To return to Becker, however, the spectre of death is integral, not antithetical, to the act of shopping. He is best known for establishing the idea that culture functions to alleviate the tragic human awareness of our own mortality. Since the 1980s, social psychologists have evolved Becker's ideas into what's known as terror management theory, a field of study grounded in the idea that people mediate their fear of death through gaining symbolic immortality. If we adhere to something beyond us – like having kids, believing in an afterlife or the virtues of a political party, getting really into investing, or buying shoes – the meaning of our lives is no longer constrained to our puny and vulnerable mortal forms.

The concept of terror management might sound super-obvious; of course we need to do *something* to make our lives feel worthwhile. When stated simply, it just seems to delineate the obvious differences between how humans and all other animals arrange themselves. To prevent life from feeling like a pointless sleepwalk toward the inevitable, we build temples and malls, we invent more interesting ways to have sex with one another.

Where the terror management field gets interesting, though, is in its experiments. Each involves the participants engaging in 'mortality salience' exercises: standardized writing and thinking prompts that have them envision, in specific detail, what will happen to them when they die. Scientists observe participants before and after envisioning their deaths to conceptualize how piquing awareness of one's mortality influences one's behaviour.

Over the past few decades, hundreds of studies have shown that when people are reminded of their death, they subconsciously take actions to affirm their cultural beliefs and assuage their anxiety. In other words, our fear of death lingers in behaviours that seem to have nothing to do with death at all. After engaging in mortality salience exercises, participants intensify their affiliation with those who share their religious beliefs and aggression toward those who don't; among many other things, they cut down more trees in a virtual logging game and, if they pre-reported that they glean their self-esteem from being a good driver, they drive more aggressively. (This study has been used to explain why car accidents, disturbingly, increase in areas that have traffic fatality tally signs.) In a culture that values materiality, these experiments naturally find the mortality salient more compelled to shop. One study found that mortality salient participants reported being distinctly more interested in buying high-status items, such as a Lexus or Rolex, than people who did not participate in mortality salience exercises. The authors suggested this indicates that luxury brands should place advertisements during television programming that makes viewers feel afraid.

I like this idea. People I already don't like – those who buy huge trucks, the rich – do what they do because they feel puny inside. I'm also tempted to apply this idea to everything – why I panic-bought so many candles during March 2020, why I started drinking more after Health Canada released guidelines advising the exact opposite, why malls exist in the first place.

In any case, terror management does offer some texture to explain why, despite being such bad hosts for memorials, malls sometimes become memorials themselves. Two developers in Michigan, for example, opened Mackie's World, the first American mall dedicated solely to children, in memory of their son, who died at the age of three; it closed in 1999, thirteen months after opening. Who can say whether the Ghermezian family or Victor Gruen got into the business of malls because they, too, had death on the mind? How could you be interested in raising a huge and expensive structure without having a serious interest in your wealth or the legacy of your genius exceeding your current form? The physical structures a person or people create have long been metaphors for their innermost state, the stability of your ego inversely related to the fortress surrounding you.

Similarly, we can consider how malls are a dream house of ideology. The grandest, most American example of this is the Oculus, the $4 billion transit and shopping hub completed in 2016 to replace the destroyed World Trade Center transit station in New York. Looming, steps away from Ground Zero's massive memorial reflective pools, the white steel structure looks like a wave, or whale teeth, or a dovetail, depending on who you ask. The architect, Santiago Calatrava, conceived of it as a phoenix, 'a testimony of hope, as a witness of belief that we can overcome this tragedy.' Controversially, the shopping experience at the centre experienced a rebirth of its own. Higher-end stores, including the likes of Stuart Weitzman and Sephora, rise from the ashes of the functional shoe-shiners and magazine kiosks that populated the old transit centre. The gentrification, the memorialization, the nationalism bubbling under it all – it feels bad. I did, however, find a YouTube tour through the space in which the guide counters the criticism. She suggests that the shopping experience supports the hopeful theme envisioned by Calatrava. 'I choose to look at this as a place of hope,' she says. 'Maybe if I get enough subscribers on my YouTube channel, I too will be able to walk into Sugarfina and eat all of the twenty-four-karat gold gummy bears that my heart desires.'

From the inside, the Oculus's phoenix wings/whale teeth resemble gothic flying buttresses. The grandness skews a straightforward reading of the space. Is it a sacred, sombre mall or a memorial desecrated by the banality of a mall? I have been inside the structure a couple of times and never know how to act. When I see people taking selfies in it, my socially concerned self stirs at the lack of decorum. This is a memorial! But that wouldn't be true, either; it is a mall, the selfies no more offensive than texting in a Starbucks. Some-one tweeted *not to be* RUDE *but I wanna* FUCK *in the Eatily in the 9/11 Memorial Oculus Mall!!!!* and this isn't entirely different from how I feel about 9/11, either; I didn't ask for any of this, this doesn't seem to have anything to do with me, so I might as well make a joke out of it.

The Oculus is hardly the first or last location to toe the line between consumerism and the sacred. In 2014, Ziauddin Sardar bemoaned the mallification of Mecca in a *New York Times* op-ed. A complex of seven hotel and super-luxury mall complexes – one among them is the world's fourth-tallest building – now dwarf the Masjid al-Haram, the sacred pilgrimage site of the Islamic faith. The spirit of shopping is a parasite to the pilgrimage's virtue.

The strangeness of the Oculus, and death in malls in general, reminds me of Anisa Mehdi's letter to the *Times* in response to Sardar's article. 'The paradox of Mr. Sardar's lament,' she writes, 'is that while people lose something of the past, they gain a 21st-century test of their faith and practice.' A mall at Mecca is conceptually strange but situationally true, Mehdi argues; it only makes explicit the threats that one must already circumvent to create spiritual meaning in one's life. Like the cognitive estrangement of science fiction, making the familiar, even the sacred, strange allows us to see the truth more clearly.

Malls become strange in death. And through becoming strange, they reveal the truth of how our lives and desires are intimately connected. Despite attempting to outrun our deaths through buying and building monuments, we will die. Despite doing everything to separate ourselves from one another, we nevertheless belong to one another; we fail each other all the time.

Frustratingly, no one has been held responsible for the Mindbender accident. And *accident* is hardly the right word for what happened – even *crash* doesn't do it justice. Technically, the roller coaster came apart before it made impact with anything. Four bolts in the final car's wheel assembly wiggled loose, which caused it to career off the track and smack into a concrete pillar. The impact disengaged the car's lap belt, which thrust Tony Mandrusiak and Cindy Sims out of their seats; David Sager and Rodney Chayko fell as the roller coaster entered the final loop.

The provincial inquiry into the accident blamed the crash on flaws in the design created by the German manufacturer, which had gone bankrupt before the roller coaster ever opened. The inquiry did also mention that the mall could have caught the loose bolts earlier, had more stringent inspection procedures been implemented.

The language we have to describe the accident all but evaporates any role a human being had in the crash – as if a machine can make mistakes independent from the people who built it. I wonder if this is why the mythology of the Mindbender has loomed so large in my hometown. Without anyone to blame, the responsibility and the threat of future catastrophe become absorbed into the building itself.

Legally, this is almost the case. West Edmonton Mall sued its insurance companies for $11 million in damages but only received $63,000. But this still dwarfs what the victims' families received. Sims's and Mandrusiak's parents claimed that the funds they got from the mall by settling out of court weren't enough to cover even half of the funeral costs. At the time, Alberta's Fatal Accidents Act limited accidental death claims to $3,000 each. The Mandrusiaks settled out of court and weren't allowed to disclose how much they received. Sims's parents left the city shortly after the accident; Mandrusiak's stayed. When the roller coaster reopened just over a year after their son died, they told the *Edmonton Journal* they were tormented by the ceaseless TV advertisements for the mall, showing people screaming, just like their son had, on the Mindbender.

The crash has been condemned to history as a true mistake rather than an inevitability baked into the roller coaster's design. To me, it also seems strange that a roller coaster could crash without a person or two getting rich from it. I came of age in the period of the early 2000s when it seemed like every other week someone was suing a fast-food company because they'd found a severed finger in their burger. I guess I've implicitly believed in some karmic justice whenever a corporate anvil falls out of the sky: it sucks, but you or your family will prosper for generations as a result.

In reality, getting to the root of a structural failure is as complicated as untangling the process – the engineering, the architecture, the business – that built the structure. No satisfying justice, for example, has been found in the ten years following the Rana Plaza collapse. When victims tried to sue Loblaws – the Canadian retailer whose Joe Fresh clothing was produced at Rana – for $2 billion, Canada's Supreme Court struck down the attempt, claiming that the Canadian company couldn't be held responsible for the safety of the factories it used. And although thirty-seven people in Bangladesh have been charged with the murder of the collapse victims, only one, the owner, is currently in custody awaiting trial. Until then, blame rests on the fact that the building was constructed on unstable land – once a body of water, it had been converted into a landfill before construction – and therefore was doomed from the start. Thanks to the bypassing of construction codes (one of which, ironically, was the land's zoning to be a shopping mall) and the use of poor-quality materials, illegal generators on the top floor, and heavy vibrating industrial sewing machines, the collapse was all but inevitable.

On the seventh anniversary of the disaster, Oxfam published a video commemorating the event, featuring testimony from a garment worker who narrowly escaped the collapse. She didn't want to work in the factory in the first place but had to – rent, school fees for her children, food. When she reported the cracks in the walls the day of the collapse, her supervisor threatened to withhold her pay; moments later, she was losing consciousness under the rubble.

The video closes with a series of vague statements on the screen – 'Standards must not be allowed to slip. Vigilance around safety must continue' – suggesting that people cared for the workers' safety in the first place or that a momentary lapse in vigilance caused the building's demise. As if the collapse was the result of a slippage and not a design.

A frustrating narrative follows Canada's most notable mall collapse. In 2012, a steel beam of a rooftop parking lot gave way, causing the Algo Centre Mall in Elliot Lake, Ontario, to fold in on itself. Nineteen injured people escaped. After scouring the site for two days, rescue crews could still detect signs of life – a muffled voice, tapping sounds – underneath the rubble, about thirty metres out of their reach. The taps were likely coming from Lucie Aylwin, who picked up a couple of shifts each month at the mall's lottery ticket kiosk to save money for her upcoming wedding. That afternoon, however, the Ministry of Labour called off the recovery effort, stating that it was too dangerous. The demands of an aggressive crowd later compelled the rescuers to keep searching and, eventually, recover the bodies of Aylwin and a second woman: the recently widowed Dolores Perizzolo, who regularly bought lottery tickets at the kiosk where Aylwin worked.

A public inquiry into the collapse revealed that the mall's construction rendered its collapse inevitable. The parkade was never watertight; the connection between the beam and a steel column had begun corroding from its construction in 1979, the result of an already faulty design and lack of maintenance on the rooftop parking lot's surface. (The frequently leaking mall earned the nickname 'Algo Falls.') The report found that all three successive owners of the mall had the resources to fix the leakage but never did, opting to patch and seal the cracks – a band-aid solution that never worked. Municipal authorities also ignored repeated complaints about the leaking ceiling.

By the time the mall collapsed, the steel beam, eroded from melted snow and road salt, had only 13 per cent of its original capacity left. A grey Ford Focus driving over the beam caused it to finally give out. In his damning report, however, Justice Paul Bélanger claimed that the collapse was ultimately caused by 'human, not material failure.' He observed a scandal of apathy, incompetence, and greed culminating in the collapse of the building. A stunning number of people in positions of power somehow forgot a basic tenet of material science: when water, air, and chlorides meet, they make rust; when steel rusts, it will not stop weakening until it disintegrates.

Bélanger's report also reveals how this grand failure is the product of the conditions surrounding it. But it all comes down to the history of Elliot Lake, Bélanger writes, namely the fact that it was first settled as a uranium mining town during the Cold War. The mall was first built to accommodate a booming population and, eventually, to give them a reason to stay after the next bust. When the last uranium mine closed in 1996, the city rebranded as a retirement destination. With this, it created a not-for-profit retirement living corporation that took on ownership of the mall from 1995 to 2005. This resulted in the mall becoming a vital source of tax revenue and employment when other sources dried up; in other words, it became a true town square, housing the library, offices of the local MPP and MP, a funeral home, a hotel, and the largest of the city's two grocery stores. Ultimately, Bélanger wrote, builders, engineers, mall owners, and local officials overlooked clear structural dangers to avoid disrupting what had become a vital business and social space in Elliot Lake. It wouldn't be dramatic to say that the closing of this mall would signal the end of a certain local world. That's the claim I want to make to rationalize how and why two women had to die because a mall fell upon them.

This mall could not have existed without the industry that preceded it; the mall wouldn't have collapsed without it, either. Uranium mining, too, could only be built by undermining another way of life. The American nuclear program demanded greater stores of the substance. Twelve mines eventually opened in the area. Uranium mining encapsulated what Anishinaabe historian Lianne Leddy calls 'Cold War colonialism'; the radiation and tailings from the mines and a sulphuric acid plant built directly on the reserve poisoned the ecosystem the Serpent River First Nation relied on to fish and trap. Establishing the industry itself was a neo-liberal policy decision of a colonial state. Entangling First Nations into the resource extraction economy and formalizing their reliance on wage labour would relieve the province of its financial treaty rights.

These three aspects are all physically captured in one obvious metaphor on Elliot Lake's waterfront. The memorials for the mall victims and mine workers are steps away from each other at the mouth of Horne Lake, a piece of the region's uranium-poisoned watershed flowing into the Serpent River First Nation thirty kilometres south. The mall wouldn't exist without this first destruction: the excavation that disrupted and all but eliminated a way of life, all for a new one that couldn't even keep its own building from eroding onto itself and two working-class women at a lottery booth. I can't believe how stupid it is, how on the nose. But I can't forget: in taking a life, the mall becomes the most important thing in the world.

———

Everything, it seems, is on the verge of collapse: ecosystems, economies, societies. The word itself comes from *collabi*, Latin for 'fall together,' so when something collapses, it doesn't just end. A collapse self-destructs. It's sudden and takes everything with it.

I am more attuned to my sense of doom when I visit home. I don't want to feel this way. I don't think it's fair or even accurate that I associate the place that I'm from with environmental destruction. I don't like how long it takes to drive from the airport to my parents' house. In the winter, I sit in my friend's car and see the pollution pluming upward and staining the snow brown.

Naturally, the second of West Edmonton Mall's iconic bronze sculptures is about oil. It was made by the same man who made *Open Sea*, the bronze whale statue, and represents three oil workers drilling a rig into the ground. Until I was tall enough to see its whole shape, I just thought it was the world's slipperiest, most boring jungle gym. I called my dad a liar when he told me what I was staring up at was supposed to be three men somehow getting the stuff that eventually goes into our car. Now it is tragic to look at, a relic of a time that will, soon enough, no longer exist.

From a different angle, the statue looks threatening – the bronze men drilling into the ground are literally disrupting the natural order of things, unnerving the earth beneath our feet. When I look at the statue, I have collapse on the mind. The mall itself is untrustworthy, too. Structures that have been built for pleasure cause human beings to die. People jump from their railings, the buildings fold onto themselves. The ceiling of a parkade at West Edmonton Mall recently collapsed. Miraculously, nobody was injured, but it can't be the last time. As with the Algo Centre, the colonial logic that built this mall is inseparable from the logic that dispossessed the land it was built upon. A bigger collapse is surely coming.

I want to distance myself from this place: my home, but the entire world where my home resides, too. I don't want to belong to somewhere so wrong and threatening.

This sense of alienation is what drew me to Mark Fisher in the first place. Unlike anyone else I had read at the time, he articulated how depression could be a social problem while being felt so deeply, often unspeakably or even embarrassingly, in the individual. I was struck by the admission in his essay 'Good for Nothing' that his 'depression was always tied up with the conviction that I was literally good for nothing.'

Fisher was convinced he had faked his way through grad school and was incompetent in office and factory jobs; while unemployed and living in the psych ward, he was convinced that he was faking it to prevent himself from working. He recognized the dizzying dissonance between having real privilege and being immobilized by disaffection. This stuck with me. I'm too privileged to feel this way – how could I possibly feel out of step within a world that has been built, at the cost of lives of others, for someone exactly like me?

What I took away from his writing was that I wasn't alone in feeling like an alien for not wanting to live in this moment in time, a feeling that has intensified with the coming social and environmental collapse. It all felt unfair, as if there were another timeline for me to live in: I belong to a world that I don't like, and I am so complicit in it that I have convinced myself I am incapable of imagining a way out. It must have been comforting to believe that the world had nothing to do with me.

Reading Fisher's essay again now, I can see that my twenty-two-year-old self read it myopically. This can't possibly be what he wanted anyone to take away from it. Depression, Fisher argues in this particular essay, is a social condition both produced by austerity and debilitating the working class's ability to organize a way out of it. However, he says, the pervasiveness of this condition is also a sign of hope: What if we could wrangle disaffectedness into anger?

I wonder if it's possible to see all this pain caused in the mall, because of the mall, and see the common experience as evidence of a potential, to see the cultural phenomenon of disconnection as a potential site for connection, as evidence of humanity. If a mall can collapse, it means that things won't be this way forever.

Future

The first year of the COVID-19 pandemic was a precarious rope-and-pulley system suspending a new version of my life above the old one. The already little work I did outside of being a grad student moved online. I got a lot of money from the government and languished over a *thesis*. I became obsessed with buying anything the internet offered (read: every imaginable derivative of weed) to strong-arm my head into focusing on writing anything for more than ten minutes. None of it worked. I stared for long hours at the wall, my phone, my face in the mirror, in an apartment that, by all accounts, was the same apartment I had lived in for years but that increasingly took the shape of a cage threatening to last forever. I wasn't miserable because I missed people but because I felt useless. I tried to remedy this by spending whole days walking in silence by the ocean. I felt Victorian, like a tubercular heiress, as if this absurdly miserable bourgeois life could make sense only in a different time. I wanted it to change but didn't think it could, materially, get any better than this. After all, I was getting paid to hardly work. A miracle. Reality was so real and so not. I could lie down in the middle of my street on a Friday night and hear metal pots and wooden spoons ringing from all the apartment buildings around my own and it always surprised me: so many people had been living here this whole time.

This is the same period when I found the Backrooms on TikTok, a genre of tours through computer-generated spaces absent of people, often resembling an office, a windowless hotel pool, or an empty mall. Each Backroom looks uncannily familiar. I became addicted to staring at them, although the discursive aura surrounding it all annoyed me. Half the comments (and the cultural metacommentary on the comments) seemed to exist for no reason beyond demonstrating the writers' understanding of the word *liminal*. The other half insisted the universally 'nostalgic' vibe emanating from the videos was proof of a simulated reality or an alternate universe, as if these ceiling tiles and fluorescent lights triggered long-repressed memories from the other side of the matrix: 'what if the back rooms is a way to escape the simulation and if u finish all the levels ur out of the simulation?'

To be fair to TikTok user @your_random_bestie, quoted above, and all the others on the same wavelength, the Backrooms are similar to dreams, amalgams of the Junkspaces our consciousness hardly registers as real places in their in-situ forms. They capture the contemporary affect of space so accurately that we think they belong to another dimension. These generated spaces are perfectly bland, with no particular markers of culture or time. Curiously, though, the most popular feeling commenters associate with the Backrooms is nostalgia.

For me, they're reminiscent of the Windows 95 maze screensaver, the now-closed lazy river at West Edmonton

Mall's waterpark, the back hallways I walked through with my grandma when she worked at Kingsway Mall in Edmonton. When I was twelve or so, she got a job at a new kitchen tools kiosk opened by my best friend's mom. It was December and the sun was setting before dinnertime, the very cold time of year when every element of life retreated even more inwardly. I spent a few school nights helping her set the place up. After the mall emptied of early Christmas shoppers, we pushed metal carts through the now dark, silent spaces and past stores behind metal security curtains, before lifting boxes of silicon spatulas and whisks from the loading dock. The gigantic, hollowed space made me aware of how insignificant and small I was. And somehow I was important enough to be one of the few inside it. This, I speculated, was what adulthood must feel like: purposeful, ordinary, alone. The Backrooms are similarly uncomfortable and thrilling.

———

The pandemic triggered a whole trend of cultural commentary on liminality. It was impossible to escape these thoughtful, descriptive, unhelpful evaluations of how our new lives felt like an empty movie theatre, a vaguely familiar hallway, the eternal underwearless moment before the doctor sees you. I couldn't stop saying the word myself. Every evening, my partner and I began walking the long, unpeopled commercial stretch of West Broadway; we wouldn't say much to each other, outside of how strange, how *liminal* it was to walk past so many empty tailor shops and restaurants. When I tried to talk to other people, what mostly came out was an attempt to capture how truly liminal my life had become and how this liminality was the specific cause of my misery. I was between school and work, fake life and real life, not really wanting to be alive, not wanting to be not alive, either. There had to be another side to this interminable middle. Defining the pandemic experience of time, over and over and over, didn't change how badly that particular experience of time sucked. But this exercise did give the time a bit of shape, if only with my mouth.

Online liminal spaces, like the Backrooms and @Space-LiminalBot on Twitter, gave external texture to my interior state of in-between-ness, the disquieting comfort of being frozen in time. This is hardly an original experience, confirmed by the online communities formed around documenting and discussing dead malls. The r/deadmalls subreddit, for example, has almost 180,000 members; people post near-identical photos of empty, death-rattling shopping centres. Certain YouTubers have made entire careers of touring shuttered and shuttering sad malls in the American Midwest. The king of dead malls, Dan Bell from Maryland, has amassed more than 600,000 subscribers that way. To avoid being busted by security for filming, he records his tours with spyglasses, which put the viewer in the first-person perspective, as if you're the one privately walking through the space.

Without people, malls are stripped down to their aesthetics. Unless you've physically been to one of these malls yourself, each dead mall could be a continuation of the last, the subreddit or Dan Bell's YouTube page just one tour of the same huge building. They contain close-enough commonalities: skylights, decaying gardens. The real hits have neon accents, teak, signage from decades ago that resisted the recent coagulation into monochrome sans-serif font. The sheer resilience of maintaining this aesthetic should be reason enough to keep these malls around. Then again, they don't look like places I would want to shop.

Dead malls, then, are empty of purpose but overflowing with meaning: an easy visual metaphor of a lost world that we only recently, stupidly loved. These worlds are individually and societally sweeping. A picture of a long-empty food court poised for demolition can stir the memory of someone who skipped school to eat lunch at that specific table as a teenager; the picture does the same for someone who ate lunch at a look-alike table on the other side of the continent. There's a shared experience in this recognition and this loss. The memory container for both, either real or symbolic, is closer to death than life – mirroring, affirming, that our own lives have departed adolescence in the same direction.

As a symbol of history or ideology, the dead mall will take just about whatever you throw at it. Like any artifact of these times, the dead mall is capital-letters Late Capitalism. The stalled escalators and flickering fluorescent lights tell a story of how our current way of economically organizing ourselves is ungracefully rotting before our eyes. Or a story of how we once believed in a system enough to build permanent infrastructure around it but can't even afford to fix it. Dead malls in rural and working-class areas represent a lost American Dream. They are very big houses possessed by the same spirit that compels a whole people to vote for Trump and die of old age while working at Walmart. On the other hand, one academic has posited that we can read the dead mall as a queer icon. If the living mall is a testament to white nuclear suburbia and neo-liberalism, the unabashedly dead one opposes that ideology: the dead mall commands you to look its way, an adamant reminder of a system failed.

Dan Bell's YouTube videos emanate a similar disaffected vibe. They are soundtracked by acidic, synthy vapourwave music, often created through remixing the neutral tones of the Muzak played in liminal spaces such as malls or elevators. Vapourwave emerged in 2010 or so as artists on online forums began sharing music and visual art that reproduced and distorted the punchy colours and sounds of the eighties. Vapourwave is distinctively of-the-internet, a digital vehicle to animate the colourful detachment of the extremely online.

In a TED Talk narrativizing his YouTube career, Dan Bell draws a parallel between vapourwave artists and the pre-internet generation that hung out in malls; both identities represented actions taken to not only express but resolve idleness in one's life: 'the whole aesthetic is a way of dealing with things you can't do anything about, like no jobs, or sitting in your parents' basement eating ramen noodles.'

A whole other niche belongs to the genre of music created to sound like it's playing in an empty mall. The videos manipulate yearnful songs from the eighties and nineties ('Africa,' 'Friday I'm in Love'); distorted with a slight echo, they project both sadness and comfort. In the *New Yorker*, Jia Tolentino has mused on the achy appeal of these videos. In some ways, she writes, they outsource the viewer's solitude; wading through a comment section abstracts us from the risk of loneliness: in public, your isolation on display for anyone else in the food court; in private, audience of one to your mind's singular loudness. In another sense, the simulated mall experience – tours of fake ones or of real ones we have never experienced – serves as a time capsule, digitally immortalized and made real among strangers. Documenting the dead mall, Tolentino writes, saves places and selves from impermanance: 'who we were and how we lived still exist, if on an altered plane – that, like the malls themselves, our pasts will resist their own erasure.'

Vapourwave, then, can be understood as a genre of yearning. What it yearns for, if we're to return to Mark Fisher one last time, is the expectation of a future. In *Ghosts of My Life*, Fisher writes that the emergence of a neo-liberal and globalized economy time-stamped the beginning of the 'slow cancellation of the future,' an uncanny feeling that became fully recognizable by the end of the twenty-first century. In the postwar period, Fisher argues, the future felt distinct from the present in a way it does not now. Emerging technologies and world order promised that something, something better, was on the horizon.

He says this distinction between past and present – and an anticipation of new sounds and styles to come – was evident in the progression of rock and pop music through the twentieth century. Consider how, if you were listening to the radio in the eighties, an artist imitating the style of Buddy Holly would either be marketed as retro or received as such. Compare that to the more seamless seepage of vintage elements in contemporary pop culture. Without any background knowledge, would you be able to place an Arctic Monkeys music video in the present day or twenty-five years earlier? Would you guess that Mark Ronson produced Amy Winehouse's *Back to Black* to echo sixties soul? As a result, the only 'futuristic' music (or art in general) of our current life is retro-futurism; popular music and TV shows and movies struggle to define themselves independently from art that was made decades ago. If we're living in the future, it doesn't feel that way.

Culture's future-collapse is partially a product of a life made more expensive, and less conducive to imagination. (What would art have become if, in the eighties, the Lower East Side was as unaffordable to working artists as it is now?) More broadly, the death of the future resulted from the snaking of the market into every area of public and private life: the ballooning profit motive for essentially all media, the way we are too tired and overstimulated and broke to seek out, let alone make, something new.

Our present is now haunted by the future. Adapting a term coined by Derrida, Fisher finds 'hauntology' lingering in art that replicates affects and aesthetics from the past – not only a longing for a future that's not coming, but for the ability to imagine it at all.

———

Watching West Edmonton Mall's commercials from its heyday is like peering into another world. One from 1986 features classic shots of absolutely stoked white people cruising in scooters and modelling power suits. A couple points at the sights on Europa Boulevard as if they're strolling down the Champs-Élysées. Overtop all of it blares a synthy power jingle with the inspiring command *Do what you want to do, be what you really want to be, and find yourself at West Edmonton Mall.*

The song and visuals are so effective that I really do begin to believe that West Edmonton Mall is a space where self-actualization is possible. But then the haunting part, the longing part, makes itself known. This distinct flavour of mall optimism is a relic of the past. I get the sense that I know something they don't, but I would still rather be them, engaging with consumerism, with life, in such a pure and unironic way.

The commercial is one of the nearly two hundred videos posted to Best Edmonton Mall, a YouTube channel launched in 2016 by diehard fan and self-anointed mall historian Matthew Dutczak. Dutczak's videos unearth every aspect of the mall's past and present: updates on new rides and slides, reviews of food court fare, history on details as minute as the designs on the road signs that once led drivers to the mall. Sometimes he hosts livestreams attended by hundreds of other mall enthusiasts, featuring trivia games and unseen footage of the mall's storage areas.

Dutczak's relationship to the mall is unlike that of anyone I have ever met. When I tell people what I've been writing a book about – or just mention – the mall, reactions swing between poles of outright rejection and ironic glee. But Dutczak's love for the mall exposes mine as performative at best. Dutczak also hosts a mini-museum of WEM memorabilia in his basement: an eleven-foot-long window shade once used in the Fantasyland Hotel, a collection of West Edmonton Mall spoons and Deep Sea Adventure shirts, a tribute to his beloved submarines. His videos, then, come from a place of fierce adoration. In an interview with a local radio station, Dutczak said he was inspired to create the channel after realizing how many Edmontonians didn't appreciate the entirety of the mall's history. (One day at work, he told a few younger co-workers that he missed the mall's submarines. They had no clue what he was talking about.)

In his videos, Dutczak speaks with the assuredness that his audience is already interested in what he's talking about. He resists the normal Edmontonian route of debating whether the mall is a good one in the first place, whether it killed downtown. In one rare video, he addresses the city's polarizing opinion of the mall, expressing genuine befuddlement that anyone could be critical about West Edmonton Mall: 'People, for some reason, like to talk about how much they don't like the mall, as if having every store you could possibly imagine, along with an amusement park, a water park, movie theatres, bowling, minigolf, a fully accredited zoo, escape rooms, ice-skating, ziplines, and over ninety different dining options all in one place – ' he pauses to gasp ' – somehow makes that a place you *don't* want to go?'

The driving emotion of his channel is nostalgia – Dutczak yearns for his childhood in the mall. In his discussion of the 1986 commercial mentioned above, for example, he can't help but comment that the World Waterpark is depicted in the better days of the eighties, when it had more trees. In a video about the new car dealership in Phase I, he quickly segues into a lament for the lost mall of his childhood, how amazing the landscaping looked back then. Dutczak's most popular videos start with the words 'What happened to … ' and revisit long-gone aspects of the mall: the bronze whale, the lazy river slide at the waterpark, the fountains in the Phase III food court. Many end on a solemn refrain, calling the viewer to *remember: remember the laser maze, shaking hands with dolphins, the submarine rides; remember the jumping water in the Phase III food court ...*

I am resistant when watching these videos, my body tensing and cocooning as if I'm walking through the section of the mall where men are pointing hair straighteners at my head or holding out bottles of perfume for me to try. Dutczak is selling a concept to me. Joy? An unironic love for my hometown? (An unironic love for literally anything?)

But then again, he has clearly tapped into something real. His videos routinely attract thousands of viewers, an enthusiastic chunk of them adding their own yearnings and stories in the comments section. They also want the submarines back, and the dolphins. Several remember the waterpark's bungee-jump tower but were never old enough to take the leap themselves before it closed for good. Some always intended to do it but kept putting it off for another time. 'Guess the lesson learned is to always grab the opportunity in your life while you can, because you never know if it will be your last one,' one viewer writes.

These demands on West Edmonton Mall's past make me sympathetic for the poor thing. Romanticizing the past just isn't politically useful, either.

A prime example lives on the r/deadmalls subreddit. One of the most commented-on posts in the subreddit was in response to a user's idea that the massive space of dead malls should be converted into housing. What followed was more than one hundred comments demonstrating an obsessive commitment to brainstorming the multiple ways in which that couldn't ever be possible: malls are isolated from the rest of the world, they're in poor condition, it would cost more money to retrofit them than what they're worth. A moderator threatened to take the post down for discussing politics despite the site's ban on anything remotely controversial. (There is at least one example of a dead mall being turned into a homeless shelter: the Carpenter's Shelter opened in an old Macy's in Virginia in 2018.) The time people spent cutting short the dead mall's potential isn't just indicative of their lost ability to visualize the future. By spending this much time retreating into the past, people eat away at any opportunity they might have at creating a better future, one that doesn't revolve around circulating profit. Mall nostalgia seems like a potentially dangerous distraction from what matters.

This is all lip service to soften how I don't have a lot of patience for people unilaterally talking about themselves. Talking about dead malls is a reflexive process: people trying to untangle what that dead mall means to them or reminds them of, individually. As when I hear other people's stories of the Mindbender crash, my eyes glaze over when I hear about the mall of an acquaintance's childhood in the depths of Washington or Manitoba or the specific things people online miss after malls go away. People on Facebook miss the Mackie's World dinosaur, people still moderate a nostalgic page of memories for the pre-collapse Algo Centre in Elliot Lake. Reading the comments on dead mall videos is about as interesting as hearing another person describe their dreams, trying to map the contours of their subconscious in real time; each has the same philosophical weight of this one below a

Dan Bell video: 'why does this fill me with both an extreme calmness but also the feeling of impending doom what the whole fuck is this.' I'm not sure why I interpret these as demands on my attention and not simply the very human thing of extending a virtual hand to connect in a lonely moment in history, in a place as lonely as the internet.

And I say all this as if I'm not also desperate to have my experience reflected back onto me. Nobody's nostalgia, after all, is as interesting as my own. Nothing will ever be as interesting to me as the fact that my grandma worked in a mall, as interesting as driving anyone I know in my parents' car around St. Albert, past my high school, the first tiny house that my family lived in. There's a desire for my passenger to understand me more; there's also a desire to go back to that time and to take them with me. My high school, full of asbestos, was knocked down this year, which I found privately devastating. I can never go back. In another way, its destruction is comforting. I will never have to risk going back and discovering the truth, which is that I no longer belong there. Instead, it will always live as an idealized space in my mind. We will belong in our mythology of a place forever.

I think this is why I love Margaritaville – I am always on a quest to find the perfect space. Consider how its gift shop is the truest place on earth, the spiritual honesty of a lawn chair declaring 'no working during drinking hours,' the power of a cartoon parrot livin' for the weekend. No element of this place shies away from its hatred of the banality of work, adulthood, and capital. The whole vibe breezily transcends the pain of modern life with the means available to most of us: a blended drink and the sweet sounds of yacht rock.

I really do wish I could be a baby boomer on vacation. What a dream: my existence beginning before things became this expensive, my natural lifespan expected to end before the earth's temperature gets personally threatening. Peace, so gentle it could be torture, rains over me.

More honestly, and more darkly, I like how Margaritaville makes me feel like I've worked hard and deserve a break. A devastating realization of the COVID-19 pandemic was that I need to feel useful but don't care very much about being that way. Margaritaville rewards me with the experience of working, hating work, and yearning for five o'clock. I want the vestiges of a social experience without being social.

This means that I have no problem identifying what I find wrong with the world. But when I think about what I truly want to do with my life, the actual changes I want to see, I just want to walk through a mall alone. Through writing these lines I realize that what I hate about the mall is being surrounded by people. And what I find appealing about a dead mall is its potential to belong to nobody but me. I resent other people's engagement with my solitude, my quiet imaginary space of what a dead mall is supposed to mean.

But as with the hair straighteners and the perfume, my resistance to engaging with Dutczak's mall is symptomatic of the truth. The truth being desire. I'd say I *want to want* the perfume, but I just want the perfume. I want everything. I want to let go of whatever's stopping me from letting the man spray perfume on me. I want to have perfume sprayed on me without owing the man anything. And if I were to love the mall, I would owe it something. If I were to love life, I would owe it something. Same goes for people, but I just don't have the time. I'm too busy becoming so perfect that nobody could ever stop themself from loving me.

———

This is why the mall is such a challenging place for me: I love and hate my own loneliness.

The mall gives me the full sensation of life without meaningful interaction with other people. There's safety in that, in a journey unbound to the unpredictability of others. And that's where the challenge comes in. I know life – my own and the broader concept beyond myself – can't be fulfilling without others in it.

At the beginning of this book, I set out to find the friction point between myself and the world; I wanted to capture the specific root of what, exactly, eats me alive about the mall, and the place that I come from, the time I come from, myself. The answer the mall has given me is isolation. How our histories, economies, jobs, and homes physically distance us from one another, sure. On a grander scale, it's how these materials, and the ideas that make these materials, isolate our realities from what feels like the essential truth: We are so implicated by one another. We can't live without each other.

Gruen's social vision of the mall, if we can take it at face value, is largely regarded as a failure. His intention to bring people together only drove them apart more rapidly. The mall, to be sure, shepherded in new faces of class and racial violence, expediting a rate of consumption that no finite planet could possibly outlive. Inside and out, malls are built to dominate, entrancing shoppers to dissociate from their material realities. They make junk out of and upon places that have supported whole worlds for millennia. Children are stolen from malls, animals are trapped in malls; malls crumble upon people in every sense. As long as there are malls, people will end their lives in here.

Maybe Gruen's vision was infected from the start – he was never shy about his desire for the venture to make him rich, to build his own individual legacy of creation. His ultimate admission late in life, though, reveals a current of truth. This mall, a destroyer of urban and human life, was not in the original design.

The mall, then, is a tale of how we all got to this place. When people play God with capital, they disappoint themselves; they ruin worlds. The mall also suggests that there is a way out. The story of malls is the story of people – it tells us that whatever our conditions have tried to stamp out, a desire to do otherwise remains.

This is evident when people lose their mall: when the mall renovates away their favourite attraction or when the mall collapses and people commune with others across the fraught divide of the internet – the grief they express in its loss, the delight in connecting, for a moment, with someone who feels the same.

I'm touched, for example, by the communion displayed when people lose a place like Morningside Mall in Scarborough, Ontario – just one of the many that, unlike West Edmonton Mall, primarily functioned as a true community space for those often neglected by the capitalist status quo. The mall, and many others like it, was traversed by a dedicated seniors' walking group, a vital social connection. The importance of mall-walking is only magnified when considering the often hostile climate and physical landscape for people who aren't able-bodied. Morningside Mall held a library branch and a community centre, the East Scarborough Storefront, visited by five thousand locals a month; among other services, it hosted a legal aid clinic and a meditation group for Tamil seniors.

Morningside, built in 1979, was a relic of a different (whiter, wealthier) Scarborough. By the time the mall was demolished in 2007, the inner suburb of Toronto was home to newcomers and others priced out of downtown. 'Once a beacon of suburban wealth,' the mall 'became the picture of suburban decay,' a 2007 *Globe and Mail* article explained, revealing how those who didn't rely on the mall came to see it. The mall, in other words, was no longer profitable. The truth was that Morningside was poisoned by a Walmart: after opening in an anchor Woolco's former spot, the store closed off its entrance to the rest of the mall. Business drained from the remaining stores before Walmart left the mall and opened a detached big-box store down the road. The strategy, known as 'de-malling,' has taken out at least ten Canadian malls like Morningside.

With the mall on its last legs, the East Scarborough Storefront was about to close its doors. More than 150 protesters, many of them racialized seniors, demonstrated in a last effort to save it. The East Scarborough Storefront eventually moved elsewhere, and its community followed suit. Nobody was there to watch the mall itself come down. The building, at the end of the day, wasn't what mattered.

After the dust settled from the mall's takedown, Morningside was replaced by a strip mall with banks, a dollar store, and, soon, a high-rise condo tower. I can't imagine how people would interact with each other, let alone protest, in the tiny boxes in the sky.

Holding a protest in the mall is difficult. But when groups amass enough power, malls are a striking site not only to focalize public attention – as spaces that symbolize and materialize injustice, malls allow protesters to intervene on social injustice at its all-encompassing root. Protests in the wake of George Floyd's murder took place in malls of car-dominated cities: Sioux Falls, Minneapolis, Dover. In 2013, the Idle No More protests staged a round dance that stretched all around the West Edmonton Mall's *Santa Maria*, encircling a larger-than-life representation of romanticized colonialism.

––––––––

When Brian Sonia-Wallace served as the Mall of America's writer-in-residence in 2017, he set up a typewriter and a sign: 'What do you need a poem about?'

His documentation of the project in his book *The Poetry of Strangers* carries the air of importance only a poet touting a typewriter can bestow upon themself. Sonia-Wallace tells tender stories of a cross-section of America, healing their masculinity, their downandoutedness, through the words he gifted to them.

When reading about his project, I need to fight my knee-jerk reaction to cringe or even make fun of such an earnest expression of desiring and fostering human connection. This probably says more about me than it does about the poet.

When I set that aside, I see a great truth in his project. He knits together the spirit of malls with the spirit of poems, both articulations of human want:

> *What is a mall but the repository*
> *of our collective desire?*
> *… And what,*
> *poetry,*
> *but the shortest distance*
> *between*
> *feeling and expression?*

Surely that collective desire is so huge and so true, so urgent, that trying to capture it on the page only reads as corny, a degree of earnestness that defies how I have always thought we should speak about a mall. The mall is not supposed to be a place of true possibility.

But malls, I have realized, are very spacious places. They can hold more than I thought possible, which might include what resembles hope.

———

Michael Townsend, an artist living in Providence, Rhode Island, discovered a spare, unused room in his local Providence Place mall – an accidental feature of the building's construction. Four years after discovering the spare room, Townsend was evicted from his home nearby. A developer inspired by the success of Providence Place had demolished his building and built a supermarket parking lot in its place.

With this unused space, the mall inadvertently provided a refuge for the artists originally kicked out of their homes in the name of development. Townsend and his group of artist friends returned to the space in the mall, just how Townsend had discovered it four years ago, a 750-square-foot collecting space for leftover screws and two-by-fours, materials used to build the mall itself. Artists moved into the guerrilla apartment, installing a water tank and the beginnings of a full kitchen and flushable toilet. In photos, it's indistinguishable from a regular apartment, furnished with warm lights, a china hutch, a couch, and a television. While living in the mall, the collective – called Trummerkind – created spoof advertisements satirizing the vague and placeless language of advertising for the real estate developments that displaced them.

The artists hid in the mall apartment for four more years before they discovered that a few items had been stolen from it. The thieves turned out to be mall security guards, who used personal items taken from the room to identify the tenants. Townsend was, not surprisingly, banned from the mall for life.

On his website, Townsend ends his narrative of living in a hole in the wall with a thank-you note to the place that housed him: 'Thank you mall. I have grown exponentially from having this opportunity and it has been a major and most valuable part of my life and imagination. In the future I hope to share some of my experiences and observations with a wider audience and can only say that living in the mall is great.'

This sentiment and this spaciousness, I think that's what malls offer us. Living in the mall – the real one, the one writ large – is quite great, in that this life is grand, extreme, large, too large to make sense of as a symbol. It only becomes real where we make it real.

I couldn't tell you when it will stop being real. I couldn't tell you what comes next, either. What I do know is that the walls will be here longer than I will; so will the gaps.

Works Cited

'5 Secrets of the Oculus NYC.' YouTube, uploaded by TheMeganDaily, 14 June, 2021, https://www.youtube.com/watch?v=clqnkbddpme.

'Alberta Mall, Not Wild, Will Be Permanent Home for Dolphins.' *Globe and Mail*, 31 Aug. 1996, p. A3.

Alexander, Vikky. *Extreme Beauty*. July 2019–January 2020, Vancouver Art Gallery, Vancouver.

'Anniversary of the Rana Plaza Factory Collapse.' YouTube, uploaded by OxfamAustralia, 23 April 2020. https://youtu.be/__wpom604ga?Si=4tmo5vrnxwlab96r.

Antonelli, Marylu. 'Teen-Age Society in Edmonton Split into a Variety of Lifestyles.' *Edmonton Journal*, 16 April 1980, p. B2.

Applegate, Katherine. 'Newbery Medal Acceptance Speech: You, My Friend, Have Potential.' *American Library Association Institutional Repository*, 2013. https://alair.ala.org/bitstream/handle/11213/7972/2013-newbery-speech.pdf.

Arnold, Tom. 'A Time to Play; A Time to Pray: At the Mall Chapel, Teens Gather, Discuss Problems and Hear the Bible.' *Edmonton Journal*, 24 May 1992, p. F2.

———. 'Sweeping Out WEM Rats No Solution.' *Edmonton Journal*, 25 May 1992, p. A1.

Augé, Marc. *Non-Places: Introduction to an Anthropology of Supermodernity*. New York: Verso, 2008.

Becker, Ernest. *The Denial of Death*. New York: Free Press, 1973.

Belanger, Paul. *Report of the Elliot Lake Commission of Inquiry: Executive Summary*. Ontario Ministry of the Attorney General, 2014.

Bell, Dan. 'Inside America's Dead Shopping Malls.' TED Talks, 2016. www.ted.com/talks/dan_bell_inside_america_s_dead_shopping_malls.

Belter, Robert. 'Note to Parents: 12-Year-Olds Shouldn't Be Hanging Out at the Mall.' *Edmonton Journal*, 3 May 2009, p. A15.

Benjamin, Walter, and Rolf Tiedemann. *The Arcades Project.* Cambridge, Massachusetts: Belknap Press, 1999.

'Black Friday Death Count.' Black Friday Death Count. blackfriday-deathcount.com.

'Black Friday Death Count.' Reddit. https://www.reddit.com/r/wtf/comments/1ri5m7/black_friday_death_count.

Clayton, Susan, et al. 'Zoo experiences: conversations, connections, and concern for animals.' *Zoo Biology*, vol. 28, no. 5 (2009): 377–397. https://doi.org/10.1002/zoo.20186.

Cohen, Stanley. *Folk Devils and Moral Panics: The Creation of the Mods and Rockers.* New York: Routledge, 2011.

Critchley, Ian. 'Diving with Dolphins: World a Nicer Place If Every Child Got as Much Attention as Animals at West Edmonton Mall.' *Edmonton Journal*, 27 June 1995, p. A11.

'Crowded Mall.' *Dream Interpretation*, 2023. www.dreaminterpret.net/mall.

'Dismaland.' YouTube, uploaded by banksyfilm, 25 Aug. 2015. www.youtube.com/watch?v=v2ng-mghqek.

Faulder, Liane. 'Moms and Dads of Mall Rats Must Answer Role Call.' *Edmonton Journal*, 25 May 1992, p. C1.

Fazzare, Elizabeth. 'Santiago Calatrava Explains How He Designed the Oculus for the Future.' *Architectural Digest*, 24 Oct. 2017. www.architecturaldigest.com/story/santiago-calatrava-explains-designed-oculus-for-future-generations.

'Find Yourself – 1986 West Edmonton Mall Commercial.' YouTube, uploaded by BestEdmontonMall, 18 April 2017. https://www.youtube.com/watch?v=dd7oh7fjd8a.

Fisher, Mark. 'Good for Nothing.' *Occupied Times*, 18 March 2014, theoccupiedtimes.org/?p=12841.

———. *Capitalist Realism: Is There No Alternative?* Zero Books, 2012.

———. *Ghosts of My Life.* Zero Books, 2013.

Forman, Erik. 'Making Black Lives Matter in the Mall of America.' *New Inquiry*, 3 June 2016. thenewinquiry.com/making-black-lives-matter-in-the-mall-of-america.

Fratty_Hearst. 'Not to be RUDE but I wanna FUCK in the Eatily in the 9/11 Memorial Oculus Mall!!!!' Twitter. 25 Jan. 2020, 10:44 AM. https://twitter.com/fratty_hearst/status/1221141706470514693.

Gelinas, Ben. 'Law and Order at West Ed: "Mall Rats" Keep Seven City Police Officers on the Run in Sprawling Shopping Centre.' *Edmonton Journal*, 11 Aug. 2008, p. A1.

George, Dianne, and Tove Reece. 'How Sad Dolphins Should Suffer to Provide Entertainment.' *Edmonton Journal*, 7 Aug. 1996, p. A9. Proquest, accessed 9 Oct. 2023.

Gosse, Edmund. 'Paradise Lost.' *Lapham's Quarterly*. www.laphamsquarterly.org/sea/paradise-lost.

Gosse, Philip H. *The Aquarium: An Unveiling of the Wonders of the Deep Sea*. London: John Van Voorst, 1854.

Gottlieb, Lori, and Guy Winch. 'Molly's Father's Suicide,' *Dear Therapists with Lori Gottlieb and Guy Winch*, encore, ep. 15, iHeart Media, 19 Nov. 2020. https://www.iheart.com/podcast/1119-dear-therapists-6885 3191/episode/encore-episode-15-mollys-fathers-74157314.

Gruen, Victor. 'Shopping Centres, the New Building Type,' *Progressive Architecture*, vol. 33, no. 6 (1952): pp. 67–109.

———. 'The Sad Story of Shopping Centres.' *Town and Country Planning*, vol. 46, no. 7, 1978, pp. 350–353.

Harvell, Lindsey A., and Gwendelyn S. Nisbett. *Denying Death: An Interdisciplinary Approach to Terror Management Theory*. New York: Routledge, 2016. https://doi.org/10.4324/9781315641393.

Hoagland, Tony. 'At the Galleria Shopping Mall.' *Poetry Magazine*, 2009. www.poetryfoundation.org/poetrymagazine/poems/52645/at-the-galleria-shopping-mall.

Holt, Gordy. 'Ivan Finally Plays Mating Game: Uptight Gorilla Makes "Great Leap Forward."' *Seattle Post*, 23 Jan. 1998, p. C1.

Howell, David. 'The Hippest Show Around: Great Music at Bargain Prices the Attraction at Roadside.' *Edmonton Journal*, 3 Aug. 1993, p. B5.

'I'd Say This Is a Legit Option!' Reddit. https://www.reddit.com/r/deadmalls/comments/q6w2bt/id_say_this_is_a_legit_option.

Jang, Brent. 'The Empire That "Papa" Built.' *Globe and Mail*, 4 Jan. 2000, www.theglobeandmail.com/news/national/the-empire-that-papa-built/article1035816.

Kingwell, Mark. 'Younger Is Better for Boys Selling Sex on Toronto Streets.' *Globe and Mail*, 2 July 1986, p. A1.

Koolhaas, Rem. *Junkspace with Running Room*. London: Notting Hill Editions, 2013.

Lagrange, Teresa C. 'The Impact of Neighborhoods, Schools, and Malls on the Spatial Distribution of Property Damage.' *Journal of Research in Crime and Delinquency*, vol. 36. no. 4 (1999): 393–422. https://doi.org/10.1177/0022427899036004003.

Leddy, Lianne C. *Serpent River Resurgence: Confronting Uranium Mining at Elliot Lake*. Toronto: University of Toronto Press, 2021.

Livingstone, I. R. 'Leave the Dolphins Where They Are.' *Edmonton Journal*, 7 Aug. 1993, p. A9.

Massoni, Kelley. '"Teena Goes to Market": *Seventeen* Magazine and the Early Construction of the Teen Girl (as) Consumer.' *Journal of American Culture*, vol. 29, no. 1 (2006): 31–42. https://doi.org/ 10.1111/J.1542-734X.2006.00273.X.

———. *Fashioning Teenagers*. Walnut Creek, CA: Left Coast Press, 2012.

Mcleod, Kim. 'Edmonton Vice: Huge Shopping Mall Home for Pimps, Punks and Drug Pushers,' *Ottawa Citizen*, 14 March 1987, p. H3.

Mcleod, Lori. 'The Ultimate Fixer-Upper.' *Globe and Mail*, 6 Oct. 2007. www.theglobeandmail.com/report-on-business/the-ultimate-fixer-upper/article18146734.

Mehdi, Anisa. 'Pilgrims in Modern Mecca: A Test of Faith.' *New York Times*, 2 Oct. 2014. www.nytimes.com/2014/10/03/opinion/ pilgrims-in-modern-mecca-a-test-of-faith.html.

Mikula, Tim. 'A Boy King in the City of Losers: Edmonton's Road to Recovery Must Begin by Doing the Humane Thing—Letting Connor Mcdavid Go Free.' *Edmonton Journal*, 4 May 2019, p. E5.

Nakashima, Ryan. 'A Decade Later, Families Mourn Mindbender Losses.' *Edmonton Journal*, 15 June 1996, p. B3.

'New Edmonton Mall Phase Wows Guests.' *Toronto Star*, 12 Sept. 1985.

Nunoda, Erin. 'I Think We're Alone Now: Dead Malls and the Queerly Unconsummated.' *Feminist Media Histories*, vol. 6, no. 4 (2020): 183–210. https://doi.org/10.1525/Fmh.2020.6.4.183.

Parker, Fawn. 'The Prescription.' *Maisonneuve*, 16 Dec. 2022, maisonneuve.org/article/2022/12/16/prescription.

Prosofsky, Evan. 'Waterpark.' *Vimeo*, 21 April 2013, https://vimeo.com/64521105.

Rose, Paul, et al. 'What's New from the Zoo? An Analysis of Ten Years of Zoo-Themed Research Output.' *Palgrave Communications*, vol. 5, no. 1 (2019). www.nature.com/articles/s41599-019-0345-3.

Rynor, Becky. 'Framed Reflections: An Interview with Vikky Alexander.' *National Gallery of Canada*, 19 Dec. 2018. www.gallery.ca/magazine/artists/interviews/framed-reflections-an-interview-with-vikky-alexander.

Sardar, Ziauddin. 'The Destruction of Mecca.' *New York Times*, 30 Sept. 2014. www.nytimes.com/2014/10/01/opinion/the-destruction-of-mecca.html.

Sonia-Wallace, Brian. *The Poetry of Strangers*. New York: Harper Perennial, 2020.

Strauss, Marina. 'Oil Sands Workers Heed the Call of the Mall.' *Globe and Mail*, 8 Feb. 2013. www.theglobeandmail.com/report-on-business/industry-news/energy-and-resources/oil-sands-workers-heed-the-call-of-the-mall/article8348734.

'Talking West Edmonton Mall History on 630 CHED Inside Sports Live from WEM!' YouTube, uploaded by BestEdmontonMall, 8 Feb. 2020. https://www.youtube.com/watch?v=xmguowhfuky.

'Teenage "Mall Rats" Taking Up Seasonal Residence in Plazas.' *Leaderpost*, 1 Sept. 1981, p. C1.

The Urban Gorilla. Directed by Allison Argo. National Geographic Explorer and ArgoFilms, 1990.

Tolentino, Jia. 'The Overwhelming Emotion of Hearing Toto's "Africa" Remixed to Sound Like It's Playing in an Empty Mall.' *New Yorker*, 15 March 2018. www.newyorker.com/culture/rabbit-holes/the-over-

whelming-emotion-of-hearing-totos-africa-remixed-to-sound-like-
its-playing-in-an-empty-mall.

Toomarian, Elizabeth Y., and Lindsey Hasak. 'Brains Are Bad at Big
Numbers, Making It Impossible to Grasp What a Million COVID-19
Deaths Really Means.' *Conversation*, 31 March 2022.
theconversation.com/Brains-Are-Bad-At-Big-Numbers-Making-It-
Impossible-To-Grasp-What-A-Million-Covid-19-Deaths-Really-
Means-179081.

Van Hoose, Eric. 'Why Shopping Malls Inspire Violence.' *Salon*, 26 Oct.
2013. www.salon.com/2013/10/26/why_so_much_violence_happens
_at_the_mall_partner.

Wertham, Fredric. *Seduction of the Innocent*. London: Museum Press, 1955.

'What Happened.' Trummerkind, trummerkind.com/mall/what_
happened.html.

'What Happened to the Iconic Window Shade in Room 438 at the Fantasyland Hotel?' YouTube, uploaded by BestEdmontonMall, 27 April
2020. https://www.youtube.com/watch?v=rs19bumxhla.

'Whiteout Conditions.' YouTube, uploaded by TheNewPornographers,
9 Aug. 2017. www.youtube.com/watch?v=v2xvw38ukei.

Acknowledgements

There would be no book without David Berry – your generosity and insight made me feel capable. Thank you, as well, to Alana Wilcox and the rest of the Coach House team for your support of this project; special thanks to Peter Norman for your rigour.

Thank you to my friends and the group chats they maintain. (Shoutout Skinny Legends, Wedges, Hottie Patrol, Mundare Giant Sausage!) Y'all keep my feet on the ground when my tendency is to feel like an alien. I'm grateful for Tara Maguire, who kept me accountable to writing my book proposal. While writing this book, I thought often of my friend, Luke Jansen – he believed in music, community, and Edmonton.

To my family, especially my parents: you've talked me down from any ledge I've found myself upon; any risk I take is possible because I know this. Thank you for all you do to support me.

To my many passionate teachers and mentors at Paul Kane High School, the University of Alberta, and the University of British Columbia: because of you, I know that art, reading, and writing are worthy ways to spend my life. And to my students: you've taught me that it's all more meaningful with other people.

Finally, Alex: thank you for being my partner in everything. I love going to the mall with you.

Kate Black's essays have been published in the *Globe and Mail*, *The Walrus*, and *Maisonneuve*. In 2020, she was selected as one of Canada's top emerging voices in non-fiction by the RBC Taylor Prize and the National Magazine Awards. She grew up in St. Albert, Alberta, and lives in Vancouver.

Typeset in Albertina and Lust.

Printed at the Coach House on bpNichol Lane in Toronto, Ontario, on Rolland paper, which was manufactured in Saint-Jérôme, Quebec. This book was printed with vegetable-based ink on a 1973 Heidelberg KORD offset litho press. Its pages were folded on a Baumfolder, gathered by hand, bound on a Sulby Auto-Minabinda, and trimmed on a Polar single-knife cutter.

Coach House is on the traditional territory of many nations, including the Mississaugas of the Credit, the Anishnabeg, the Chippewa, the Haudenosaunee, and the Wendat peoples, and is now home to many diverse First Nations, Inuit, and Métis peoples. We acknowledge that Toronto is covered by Treaty 13 with the Mississaugas of the Credit. We are grateful to live and work on this land.

Edited by David Berry
Cover design by David Gee
Interior design by Crystal Sikma
Author photo by Victoria Black

Coach House Books
80 bpNichol Lane
Toronto ON M5S 3J4
Canada

mail@chbooks.com
www.chbooks.com